3/16

LIVING
HISTORY

Life During
the Crusades

Other titles in the *Living History* series include:

Life During
the Crusades

Stuart A. Kallen

ReferencePoint
Press®

San Diego, CA

© 2015 ReferencePoint Press, Inc.
Printed in the United States

For more information, contact:
ReferencePoint Press, Inc.
PO Box 27779
San Diego, CA 92198
www.ReferencePointPress.com

LIBRARY OF CONGRESS CATALOGING-IN-PUBLICATION DATA

Kallen, Stuart A., 1955–
  Life during the Crusades / by Stuart A. Kallen.
    pages cm. -- (Living history series)
  Includes bibliographical references and index.
  ISBN 978-1-60152-720-2 (hardback) -- ISBN 1-60152-720-9 (hardback) 1. Crusades--Juvenile literature. 2. Civilization, Medieval--Juvenile literature. I. Title.
  D157.K36   2014
  909.07--dc23
                                                                    2014021044

Contents

Foreword

History is a complex and multifaceted discipline that embraces many different areas of human activity. Given the expansive possibilities for the study of history, it is significant that since the advent of formal writing in the Ancient Near East over six thousand years ago, the contents of most nonfiction historical literature have been overwhelmingly limited to politics, religion, warfare, and diplomacy.

Beginning in the 1960s, however, the focus of many historical works experienced a substantive change worldwide. This change resulted from the efforts and influence of an ever-increasing number of progressive contemporary historians who were entering the halls of academia. This new breed of academician, soon accompanied by many popular writers, argued for a major revision of the study of history, one in which the past would be presented from the ground up. What this meant was that the needs, wants, and thinking of ordinary people should and would become an integral part of the human record. As British historian Mary Fulbrook wrote in her 2005 book, *The People's State: East German Society from Hitler to Honecker,* students should be able to view "history with the people put back in." This approach to understanding the lives and times of people of the past has come to be known as social history. According to contemporary social historians, national and international affairs should be viewed not only from the perspective of those empowered to create policy but also through the eyes of those over whom power is exercised.

The American historian and best-selling author, Louis "Studs" Terkel, was one of the pioneers in the field of social history. He is best remembered for his oral histories, which were firsthand accounts of everyday life drawn from the recollections of interviewees who lived during pivotal events or periods in history. Terkel's first book, *Division Street America* (published in 1967), focuses on urban living in and around Chicago and is a compilation of seventy interviews of immigrants and native-born Americans. It was followed by several other oral histories including *Hard Times* (the 1930s depression), *Working* (people's feelings about their jobs), and his 1985 Pulitzer Prize–winning *The Good War* (about life in America before, during, and after World War II).

In keeping with contemporary efforts to present history by people and about people, ReferencePoint's *Living History* series offers students a journey through recorded history as recounted by those who lived it. While modern sources such as those found in *The Good War* and on radio and TV interviews are readily available, those dating to earlier periods in history are scarcer and often more obscure the further back in time one investigates. These important primary sources are there nonetheless waiting to be discovered in literary formats such as posters, letters, and diaries, and in artifacts such as vases, coins, and tombstones. And they are also found in places as varied as ancient Mesopotamia, Charles Dickens's England, and Nazi concentration camps. The *Living History* series uncovers these and other available sources as they relate the "living history" of real people to their student readers.

Important Events

638
The Muslim ruler Umar takes control of Jerusalem.

1187
The Egyptian sultan Saladin defeats the Christian king of Jerusalem and takes control of the city.

1095
On November 27 Pope Urban II preaches a sermon in Clermont, France, calling for the First Crusade to conquer Jerusalem for the Christian church.

1144
The Muslims capture the Turkish city of Edessa.

600 ••• 1000   1100

1054
The Christian church splits into two factions, the Roman Catholic (or Latin) Church, based in Rome, and the Greek (or Eastern) Orthodox Church, based in Constantinople.

1099
The First Crusade ends with Christians wresting control of the Holy Land from Muslim rulers.

1147
The Second Crusade is launched to recover the city of Edessa, but the effort ends in failure.

1146
Turkish ruler Nur al-Din spreads the idea of waging jihad, or holy war, against Christian rulers in the East.

of the Crusades

1189
The Third Crusade is launched to defeat Saladin. It ends three years later with a truce.

1203
In the first siege of Constantinople, crusaders reinstate Emperor Isaac II and make his son, Alexius IV, coemperor.

1204
When Alexius IV is overthrown and murdered, the crusaders launch another assault on Constantinople, plundering the city and murdering thousands of it citizens.

1261
Greek soldiers defeat Latin rulers in Constantinople, retaking the city for Byzantium.

1200

1250

1202
About ten thousand crusaders gather in Venice to launch the Fourth Crusade.

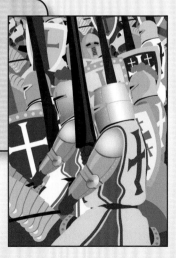

1272
The final major crusade ends, with Mamluk forces killing thousands of Christians and ending all European claims in the Holy Land.

1198
Newly elected Pope Innocent III calls for a Fourth Crusade to defeat Egypt and reclaim Christian control of Jerusalem.

Introduction

What Were
the Crusades?

In November 1095 thousands of people from across western Europe assembled in a chilly field outside Clermont in central France. The excitement in the air was comparable to a modern revival meeting or rock concert. Pope Urban II, who had traveled all the way from Rome, stood on a raised platform. The pope preached a rousing sermon that called for a holy war, or crusade.

Urban told the assembled church officials, aristocrats, knights, and peasants why a crusade was necessary. He lamented that Muslims had taken the city of Jerusalem, a city holy to all Christians. The pope claimed the Muslims were desecrating the Holy Sepulchre, the tomb that had held the body of Jesus Christ. Urban explained that a tribe of fierce Muslim warriors, the Seljuk Turks, was threatening the thousands of Christians who regularly made pilgrimages to the Holy Land of Palestine (present-day Israel).

The pope urged the knights standing before him to launch a crusade—to march off to holy war and establish Christian rule over Jerusalem. The crowd fervently responded, chanting, "God wills it! God wills it! God wills it!"[1]

Urban did not know that his call to crusade would start a series of destructive holy wars that would last nearly two centuries and kill 2 million people. Before the wars ended in 1291, there were seven major crusades and several minor ones. During those expeditions, "God wills it!" was the battle cry for Christians.

During the Crusades, the Christian church itself was divided into two factions. In 1054 the Roman Catholic (or Latin) Church split from the Greek (or Eastern) Orthodox Church. The Latin church was based in Rome and led by the pope. The Eastern church was centered in Constantinople (present-day Istanbul, Turkey), capital of the Byzantine Empire—which at the time covered much of Turkey. The Eastern church was controlled by the Byzantine emperor and led by religious leaders called patriarchs.

The split between East and West, called the Great Schism, was the result of centuries of turmoil in which the power of the Orthodox church was challenged by the Latin church. By the sixth century the Eastern and Western branches of Christianity clashed over matters of theology and even language; the official language of the Eastern church was Greek, whereas Western priests held services in Latin.

A Call to War

Although the church was split between East and West, it was united in the belief that Christians should make pilgrimages to the Holy Land. The pilgrimages were an important aspect of Christianity; those who made the journey were told that their sins would be forgiven and they would be allowed into heaven when they died. Pilgrims regularly made the trip to Jerusalem, even though Muslims had ruled Palestine since 638. Muslims and Christians shared the holy city, mostly peacefully. By the early eleventh century, every year about twelve thousand European Christians made the pilgrimage to Jerusalem.

> **WORDS IN CONTEXT**
> **Holy Sepulchre**
> Sometimes spelled Holy Sepulcher, the tomb in Jerusalem where Christians believe the body of Jesus was laid after his death on the cross.

The peaceful situation for the Christian pilgrims changed with the arrival of the Seljuk Turks. The powerful Seljuk clan from central Asia converted to Islam around 985 and took control of present-day Iraq and Iran in 1055. The brutal Seljuk warlord Tughrul Beg became the sultan of Baghdad in 1055, which gave him control over a large portion of the Muslim world. Beginning in 1064 the Seljuks began expanding their territory westward into the Byzantine Empire. In 1071 the Byzantine army was decisively defeated at the battle of Manzikert in Anatolia, a region that makes up most of the modern-day state of Turkey.

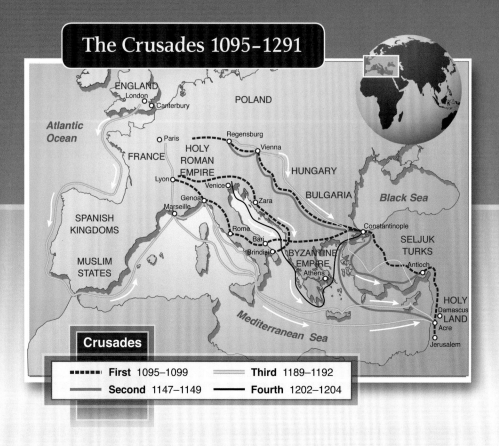

The Crusades 1095–1291

ENGLAND
London
Canterbury

POLAND

Atlantic
Ocean

Paris
Regensburg

FRANCE
HOLY
ROMAN
EMPIRE

Vienna

HUNGARY

Lyon

Venice

BULGARIA

Black Sea

Genoa
Marseille

Zara

SPANISH
KINGDOMS

Rome
Bari

Constantinople

SELJUK
TURKS

Brindisi

MUSLIM
STATES

BYZANTINE
EMPIRE
Athens

Antioch

Mediterranean Sea

HOLY
Damascus
LAND
Acre
Jerusalem

Crusades

······ First 1095–1099	═══ Third 1189–1192
── Second 1147–1149	── Fourth 1202–1204

The Byzantine Empire relied on the Anatolia heartland as a major recruiting ground for its soldiers. Once Anatolia fell to the Muslim Turks, Byzantium was no longer viewed as the major military power it had been for centuries. The lands of the once-great Byzantine Empire were reduced to the area immediately around Constantinople. Although the Turks did not attempt to conquer the city, the Manzikert defeat prompted a minor civil war among Byzantine leaders, whose struggle for control further weakened the city of Constantinople.

European leaders viewed the Byzantine Empire as a buffer between the Latin West and the Muslim East. There was panic in the West after the loss at Manzikert and further alarm when the Seljuks took control of Jerusalem in 1077. Christians feared that the Turks would deny pilgrims access to the Holy Land. While this did not happen directly, pilgrimages became much more costly and physically dangerous. At the time, many pilgrims passed through Anatolia, which was now in hostile hands. In nearly every town and village, petty Turkish rulers demanded money from pilgrims to ensure safe passage. The breakdown of government authority in the countryside allowed numerous bandits to prey on Christian travelers as they made their journey east.

A Medieval World War

The battle of Manzikert is seen as one of the root causes of the Crusades. When Urban gave his speech in 1095, he was responding to pleas from Byzantine emperor Alexius I for Western help in fighting the Seljuk Turks while reconquering Jerusalem. However, in the decades that followed, the Crusades turned into what might be viewed as a medieval world war. It was fought by people of many nationalities over a wide swath of territory.

The Christian crusading army was made up of trained knights and unskilled peasants. During two centuries and seven crusades, fighters were recruited from present-day France, Germany, Italy, Spain, Greece, England, Denmark, Norway, Russia, Poland, Hungary, and Croatia. The Muslim armies consisted of soldiers from Palestine, Syria, Jordan, Turkey, Iraq, Iran, Egypt, and elsewhere in the Middle East.

Although the Crusades were launched to control Jerusalem, major battles between Christians and Muslims occurred in Egypt, Palestine, Lebanon, Syria, and the cities of Antioch and Edessa in Turkey. Minor crusades were fought in Spain, Estonia, Croatia, Sicily, Poland, and Russia. There were also clashes on European soil when crusaders ransacked cities in Germany and fought soldiers in Hungary on their journey to Jerusalem.

> **WORDS IN CONTEXT**
> **pilgrimage**
> A journey to a sacred place or shrine undertaken as an act of devotion.

Religious Zeal

Fighters on both sides of the holy wars were driven by a combination of religious and secular desires. Christians were promised forgiveness for their sins and a place in heaven if they joined the Crusades. Muslims believed that they would find rewards in heaven for waging holy war against Christians.

Crusaders were also promised material benefits. These privileges were clearly defined, and many had legal implications. Crusaders were exempt from tolls and taxes, forgiven certain debts, and ensured speedy settlement of court cases. Knights and soldiers who survived a crusade and returned home were treated as heroes who might obtain lands and prestige that would have otherwise been denied them. In addition, crusaders retained treasures, called booty, they plundered along the way. Booty included gold chalices, jewels, and fine garments made of precious cloth.

Millions of Europeans answered the call to crusade, leaving their mundane lives behind to participate in an adventure that promised both personal enrichment and spiritual glory. However, most experienced hell on earth after they joined the Crusades. And the battles between Christians and Muslims illustrated that there was little glory to be found in the brutality of medieval war.

Chapter One

Clash of Cultures

During the Crusades two of the world's major religions, Christianity and Islam, battled for control over the Holy Land. Religion was the main justification for the wars, with both Christians and Muslims advocating violence in the name of God. Priests in churches and imams in mosques convinced their followers that fighting for their faith would guarantee them passage into heaven.

Holy warriors on both sides believed fighting for control of Jerusalem, in modern-day Israel, was the highest calling they could answer. The Bible referred to Jerusalem as the center of the world. The city fired the spiritual imagination of Christians, who believed Jerusalem was the place where Jesus was crucified and resurrected. Muslims also found the city supremely holy. They believed the founder of their religion, Muhammad, visited Jerusalem in 621 and was transported to heaven on what is called his Night Journey. During this mystical experience, Muhammad encountered the biblical figures Abraham, Moses, and Jesus and received revelations.

A Violent World

When Pope Urban II launched the First Crusade in 1095, western Europe was a wild land filled with uncultivated fields and untamed woodlands. Paris was the largest city in Europe, with about twenty thousand residents. Most other major towns had fewer than five thousand people. The only good roads in Europe were centuries old, built by soldiers of imperial Rome, a world power that ruled until the fifth century CE. In the eleventh century Europe had no central government or military authority to provide stability to society.

Violence was a constant threat to medieval Europeans, who were continually tormented by bands of marauding outlaws who raped, robbed, and murdered. Petty aristocrats built their own small armies to fight off the bandits, but wealthy nobles most often used their soldiers to fight one another. Nobles battled over scarce economic resources—land, crops, livestock, and peasant workers called serfs.

Society accepted brutal torture as the best way to punish enemies and wrongdoers. Every large estate had its own dungeon and torture chamber. Pain was inflicted on criminals, religious opponents, and political rivals by professional torturers who used barbaric methods designed to make victims suffer for as long as possible.

Suffering Serfs

Although aristocrats made up only about 5 percent of society, they sat atop an economic system called feudalism in which land was the source of nearly all wealth. Destitute serfs worked on large estates called fiefs. Feudal law required peasants to kneel before wealthy lords and swear loyalty to them in exchange for protection and the right to farm a portion of the lord's land.

Serfs lived in one-room homes constructed of wattle and daub, small tree branches woven together and covered with mud. Homes had dirt floors and small holes for windows. Food was cooked over a central hearth that left everything smelling like wood smoke. Most serfs possessed only a few cooking pots, farming tools, and rags that they wore for clothing. Serfs worked from dawn to dusk six days a week, tilling the soil while struggling to feed their families. They were required to turn over more than half their crops to the lord and also work three days a week directly for him.

The Medieval Church

While powerful landowners controlled the daily lives of European peasants, the Roman or Latin Christian church dominated the spiritual lives of all. As British Crusades historian Jonathan Phillips explains, "It is

Crusaders loot Jerusalem shops and homes after capturing the city in 1099. Christian and Muslim holy warriors believed they were fulfilling a sacred duty by fighting for control of Jerusalem.

often difficult to grasp the centrality of religious belief to medieval men and women. God's favor dictated much of their lives and explained many events, both natural and man-made. . . . Only when this is understood can we begin to comprehend episodes such as the crusades."[2]

The eleventh century was an intensely religious age. Virtually everyone attended church on Sundays and on numerous other religious holidays such as Easter, Pentecost, and Christmas. People took their babies to the church to be baptized, were married in the church, and were buried in the local churchyard.

The church had its own lands, laws, and taxes and was one of the few stable institutions in medieval Europe. Nearly every village had a church, and priests had considerable influence over the masses. The parish priest could force people to attend church and punish them if they refused. Priests also collected a tax called a tithe. Serfs were required to give a 10 percent tithe of whatever they produced to the church. Tithes were paid in seeds, harvested grain, vegetables, livestock, meat, cheese, and even bread and beer. Peasants were also required to pay for baptisms, weddings, and burial of the dead.

A Dark and Bottomless Abyss

To appreciate the power the church held over people's lives, it is important to understand the widely held belief in sin. Christians believed that they were born in sin and lived in sin. The list of sins included lust, greed, violence, and even eating too much, or gluttony. In weekly sermons, priests assured those who did not repent, or atone, for their sins that they would spend eternity in hell. Historian Will Durant explains the medieval view of hell, which was based on the writings of the sixth-century Pope Gregory the Great:

> Hell is no mere phrase; it is a dark and bottomless subterranean abyss created from the beginning of the world; it is an inextinguishable fire, corporeal [physical] and yet able to sear soul as well as flesh; it is eternal, and yet it never destroys the damned, or lessens their sensitivity to pain. And to each moment of pain is added the terror of expected pain, the horror of witnessing the tortures of loved ones also damned, the despair of ever being released, or allowed the blessing of annihilation.[3]

Even those not condemned to hell would suffer. Christian doctrine states that every soul needed to be purified before entering heaven. This meant a trip to purgatory after death. In purgatory people were punished for their sins for an indefinite period.

A Violent World

When the Christian church deemed that crusaders would be absolved of their sins and thereby granted a place in heaven, the appeal was great. Medieval society was sinfully violent, marked by petty wars, vigilante justice, and a thirst for blood that is inconceivable to most modern observers. Marcus Bull, a professor of medieval studies, explains:

> Around the time of the First Crusade it was becoming increasingly common for convicted felons to suffer death or mutilation, a departure from the traditional emphasis on compensating the victims or their families. Vendettas within and between [families] were frequent. Seldom neatly contained aristocratic combats, they had wide repercussions, for crude but effective economic warfare was regularly waged on opponents' assets, and that meant peasants, livestock, crops, and farm buildings.
>
> Brutality was so common it could be ritualistic. In about 1100, for example, a knight from Gascony [France] prayed at the monastery of Sorde that God would enable him to catch his brother's murderer. The intended victim was ambushed, his face was mutilated, his hands and feet were cut off, and he was castrated. In this way his prestige, his capacity to fight, and his dynastic prospects were all irreparably damaged. Moved by feelings of gratitude for what he believed had been divine assistance, the avenging knight presented his enemy's bloodstained armor and weapons as a pious offering to the monks of Sorde. These they accepted. This case is one small but revealing illustration of the medieval Church's inability to distance itself from the violent world around it.

Quoted in Jonathan Riley-Smith, ed., *The Oxford Illustrated History of the Crusades*. Oxford: Oxford University Press, 1995, p. 15.

Sinners could, however, avoid the punishments of purgatory or hell. Sinners could repent by confessing their sins to a priest. The regretful, or repentant, sinner who confessed was asked to sacrifice, or do penance. People fasted, prayed, or gave alms (donations) to the church to atone for their sins.

During the Middle Ages, the church also sold indulgences to those who could afford them. Indulgences were monetary payments that were said to absolve the buyer of past sins and release him or her from purgatory after death.

When Urban launched the First Crusade, he provided sinners with another way to atone for their sins. They could wage "penitential war." This involved marching to Jerusalem and waging holy war against Muslims in exchange for penance. The pope declared, "Whoever from devotion alone, and not for the purpose of gaining honors and wealth, shall set out for the liberation of the Church of God at Jerusalem, that journey will be reckoned in place of all penance."[4]

Freeing the Serfs

In addition to freeing crusaders from their sins, the pope offered material rewards. Serfs who joined the crusade were no longer required to work for their lord. The pope also promised that the church would protect the property of any crusader while he was away and help feed and clothe his family.

The pope added other extraordinary measures to motivate crusaders. They were exempt from taxes. Those who owed money were freed from paying interest on the loans. Prisoners who promised to march to Jerusalem were freed, and those who were condemned to death had their sentences commuted to life service in Palestine. Finally, the pope commanded an end to all violence between Christians. As Durant writes, the pope's measures inspired people of all classes to join the crusade:

Thousands of vagrants joined in the sacred tramp. Men tired of hopeless poverty, adventurers ready for brave enterprise, younger

Standard bearers, drummers, and trumpeters rally a Saracen (or Muslim) army. European clerics demonized the fighters they called Saracens and, with little in the way of proof, accused them of committing horrific crimes.

sons hoping to carve out [estates] for themselves in the East, merchants seeking new markets for their goods, knights whose enlisting serfs had left them laborless, timid spirits shunning taunts of cowardice, joined with sincerely religious souls to rescue the land of Christ's birth and death.[5]

Demonizing Enemies

When the pope promised to forgive the sins of crusaders, while freeing them from their feudal obligations to lords, it created what historian Norman P. Zacour calls "religious hysteria."[6] People sold all their belongings and took to the roads with no plans for survival in the harsh mountains and deserts that divided Europe from the Holy Land. Others went further. When Urban urged crusaders to "take up the cross" and sew fabric crosses to their tunics, countless men branded crosses on their bodies with red-hot irons.

Numerous clerics whipped up the fires of religious hysteria through propaganda meant to demonize the enemy. Muslims were called wicked pagans and infidels. Priests painted crusaders as members of God's army, whereas the enemy was said to be fighting for the devil. All Muslims, whether they were Arab, Persian, Turk, or African, were referred to as Saracens, a derogatory term of unknown origins. With little proof, clerics accused Saracens of rape, murder, and blasphemy (showing disrespect to God). Religious scholars spread the hatred, demonizing Arabs and robbing them of human attributes. A typical passage, by the Benedictine monk Orderic Vitalis, stated, "The detestable Saracens, permitted by divine justice, have crossed the borders of the Christians and invaded the holy places; they murdered the Christian inhabitants, and polluted the holy objects abominably with their filth."[7]

> **WORDS IN CONTEXT**
>
> **penance**
> The repentance of sins.

The Arab East

Driven by religious hysteria and hatred of the enemy, tens of thousands of crusaders marched off to the Holy Land. The crusaders were referred to as Franks, a term that defined people from France and Germany but was used by Muslims to identify all European crusaders. Few crusaders had ever been more than a day's walk from home. When they reached Arab cities, they must have been overwhelmed by what they saw.

Unlike Europe at the time, the Arab East was a thriving center of trade, agriculture, and industry. While most Europeans had little access to money, coins, or currency, Arabs bought and sold goods with a widely circulated common currency called the dinar. Arab businesses relied on windmills and water mills to power a variety of factories that produced steel, ships, food, ceramics, weapons, and lumber.

Cairo, Egypt, was known for its fine-quality cotton, silk, rugs, tents, saddles, pottery, metalwork, and gold and silver jewelry. Damascus and Aleppo in Syria produced woven fabric, stained glass, sugar, and paper. These goods were traded between regions and sold with products imported from Africa, India, and China. The Muslim geographer Muhammad al-Idrisi described markets of Damascus in the mid-twelfth century:

> The city of Damascus is filled with all manner of good things, and the streets of various craftsmen, with merchants selling all sorts of silk and brocade of exquisite rarity and wonderful workmanship—all this, such that the like exists nowhere else. . . . Also there are various kinds of fruits, which for sweetness you will not find the like elsewhere. . . . The inhabitants of Damascus have the most plentiful means of livelihood and all they require. The craftsmen of the city are in high renown, and its merchandise is sought in all the markets on earth.[8]

These prosperous markets provided merchants, traders, and artisans with an amazing array of goods. Their homes were filled with divans, stuffed pillows, lace, brightly colored mosaics, wrought copper dishes, ivory boxes, and fragrant spices. Women wore fine muslin and bracelets of gold, silver, and copper. Compared to the average Frankish crusader, these Arab citizens lived like kings and queens.

Preaching and Admonishing

With its business-driven economy, the Muslim world had the highest literacy rate of any medieval society. Centuries before the invention of the printing press, handwritten paper books were commonly available. Muslim children were also required to study and memorize the Koran, the holy book of Islam. The teachings of the Koran were studied at religious schools, or madrassas, throughout the Muslim world.

A Muslim cleric teaches his students. In contrast to other, mostly illiterate cultures of medieval times, the Muslim world had a high rate of literacy.

During the twelfth century, when 90 percent of Europeans were illiterate, Baghdad alone had thirty religious universities. Damascus was known as a school city due to its numerous madrassas, which were also found in great number in Cairo and Alexandria, Egypt. These schools also taught the Hadith, collections of stories, deeds, and sayings attributed to the Prophet Muhammad.

Narrations in the Hadith form the basis of Islamic sacred law known as sharia, which covers most aspects of family, social, and economic life. Scholars, or ulamas, and religious leaders called imams were defenders of sharia. The Spanish Muslim chronicler Ibn Jubayr described them as those "who were versed in the science of tradition, and . . . who ceaselessly admonished their followers to do right. Indeed, in the pursuit of preaching and admonishing, in warning and reprimanding, in constantly forewarning and reproving, they have attained such high stations as would win for them enough of the mercy of God to decrease their burden of sin."[9]

Sharia required public prayer five times a day; giving alms, or donations to the mosque; and fasting during Ramadan, the ninth month of the Islamic calendar. Muslims were required to make at least one pilgrimage during their lifetime to Mecca and Medina, Islam's two holiest cities. (Jerusalem was considered the third-holiest city by Muslims.) Sharia law also required believers to defend their faith. This was done by waging jihad, a term that defines the religious duty to struggle against persecution and oppression. A type of duty called jihad of the sword was the force that drove Muslims to fight Christian crusaders. In the tenth century the respected Islamic sharia scholar Ibn Abi Zayd al-Kayrawani defined jihad of the sword:

> It is preferable not to begin hostilities with the enemy before they have been invited to embrace the religion of God, unless the enemy attacks first. They have the choice of either converting to Islam or paying the poll tax. Failing either, war will be declared against them. . . . There is no prohibition against killing white non-Arabs who have been taken prisoner. But no one may be executed who has been granted the *aman* [promise of protection]. . . . Women and children must not be executed, and the killing of monks and rabbis must be avoided unless they have taken part in the fighting. Women who have participated in the fighting may also be executed.[10]

In Their Own Words

Damascus and the Valley of Violets

Around 1154 the Muslim geographer Muhammad al-Idrisi wrote a glowing account of the city of Damascus:

> Damascus is the most beautiful city of Syria, the finest in situation, the most temperate in climate, and most fertile in soil, having the greatest variety of fruits, and the most abundance of vegetables. The greater part of the land here is fruitful, and the most portion rich. Everywhere is seen the plain country, and the houses are built high. . . . From the western gate of Damascus goes the Valley of Violets, the length of which is 12 miles, and the breadth 3 miles. . . . Five streams run through it, and in every one of its domains are from one to two thousand inhabitants. . . . There are grown here all sorts of fruits, so that the mind cannot conceive the variety, nor can any comparison show what is the fruitfulness and excellence thereof, for Damascus is the most delightful of all God's cities in the whole world. The waters of the Ghautah [plain] come down in part from a spring up in the mountains. The waters burst out high in the mountains-flank like a great river, making a frightful noise and a great rushing which you may hear from afar. . . .
>
> The water of the river ramifies [branches] through all the city, and over its main stream is a bridge which the people cross. From the riverside go the markets, and water is conducted to all parts of the city, entering houses and baths and the markets and the gardens.

Quoted in Guy Le Strange, *Palestine Under the Moslems*. Charlestown, MA: Acme Bookbinding, 2003, pp. 237–38.

Sharia law was sometimes used to exert rigid control over society. When Seljuk Turkish Muslims took control of Jerusalem in 1071, religious leaders banned music, dancing, alcoholic beverages, and games. Christians were also persecuted, as fifteenth-century Egyptian historian al-Maqrizi explains: "The Christians were ordered to dress in black and to hang wooden crosses from their necks, half a meter long half meter wide. . . . They were forbidden to ride horses and allowed to ride only mules or donkeys. . . . Several people were flogged for playing chess. Churches were destroyed and their contents pillaged."[11]

The Crusader Kingdoms

Stories of Christians being abused by Turkish Muslims in Jerusalem spread throughout western Europe. Clergymen repeated the tales at church and used them to rally public support for the First Crusade against the Muslims who had conquered the city four centuries earlier. After the Christians took back Jerusalem in 1099, the victory was seen as a divine miracle in the West. For many Europeans, only the hand of God could explain the crusaders' victory over the Saracens. If the crusaders had failed, it might have signaled the end of the Crusades. However, the triumph inspired a new form of penitential warfare, which set off a protracted cycle of violence, vengeance, and reconquest that lasted decades.

> **WORDS IN CONTEXT**
> **blasphemy**
> The act of insulting or showing lack of reverence for God, religion, or clergy.

Ironically, both sides in the Crusades were driven by the same belief, as medieval history professor Thomas Asbridge writes, "In the case of Latin Christian crusades and Islamic jihad this 'public' warfare was imbued with a compelling religious dimension. . . . [Crusaders] may have had an eye for earthly profit, yet, just like other participants in these holy wars, they seem to have been moved by a heartfelt desire to attain a spiritual reward."[12]

Chapter Two

Crusaders March to the Holy Land

Throughout 1096 powerful clerics and princes of Europe organized a holy army that included about ten thousand horse-mounted knights and forty-five thousand foot soldiers, along with tens of thousands of civilians. But the crusaders were not gathered in one place. They assembled in large and small groups throughout western Europe and planned to reach Jerusalem by various routes on land and by sea. Whether they were aristocratic nobles or peasant men, women, and children, the crusaders faced similar challenges.

The holy pilgrimage to Jerusalem and other cities in the East was fraught with peril. Even the most experienced soldiers must have dreaded what lay before them. Travelers faced exposure to the elements, sickness, and starvation. The route was populated by merciless thieves and corrupt local officials, who demanded bribes, tolls, and taxes for safe passage.

Only about one-third of the original crusaders survived the 2,000-mile (3,219 km), three-year journey to the Holy Land. Those who did make it arrived exhausted and hungry. Sapped of their strength, they confronted a fierce enemy with exhaustive resources and an intimate knowledge of the local terrain.

Sorrow and Songs

Most crusaders did not expect ever to return home. Before setting out they put their affairs in order. They made out wills and attempted to repent for their sins by making peace with enemies. Many sold off their belongings to raise the funds needed for the journey. Some simply left with nothing more than the clothes on their backs, praying that God would sustain them when they exhausted their meager supplies.

Many crusaders were sorrowful about leaving their wives and families behind. A chronicler of the First Crusade, Fulcher of Chartres, wrote about a man leaving his wife: "He commended her to the Lord, kissed her lingeringly, and promised her as she wept that he would return."[13] Another French crusader wrote that his wife mourned him as if he were already dead.

During the crusading era, there were so many tearful farewells that sorrowful parting became an ingrained part of European culture. By the thirteenth century wandering minstrels called troubadours sang numerous songs about lovers leaving for the Crusades. One popular song put words in the mouth of the girl left behind: "O, when they cry 'Overseas', dear God, help the pilgrims for whom I tremble, for the Saracens are bad."[14]

Other songs dealt harshly with those who refused to pick up the cross and march into battle. Around 1149 one of the earliest troubadours, Marcabru of France, used his poetic wit to insult and dishonor those who refused to leave home and join the fight: "The lecherous wine-swillers, dinner-gobblers, fire-huggers, roadside-squatters will stay within the place of cowards; it is the bold and healthy whom God wishes to test. . . . The others will guard their own dwellings and will find a very difficult obstacle; that is why I send them away to their shame."[15]

> **WORDS IN CONTEXT**
> **troubadours**
> Traveling musicians who wrote and sang epic songs about glorious knights, romantic love, far-off lands, and current events.

The Wild Road to Jerusalem

After saying their weepy good-byes, crusaders either traveled as individuals, in small bands, or in large groups. Each style of travel had its advantages. Individuals and small groups could travel fast and had an advantage when it came to obtaining shelter and sufficient food and water. Large crowds were safe from bandits and were often financed by local churches and aristocrats.

Thousands of men leave their homes and families behind as they embark on a Crusade. Those who traveled in large groups such as this often found safety in numbers.

Whatever the size of the group, the crusaders picked routes east based on risk factors that included weather, geography, and the hostility of locals along the way. Most of the countryside was untamed wilderness. Few towns existed, and roads were nothing more than cattle trails, swamped in waist-deep mud during storms. Freezing mountains in the winter and burning deserts in the summer created nearly insurmountable obstacles.

The numerous hardships experienced by French count Raymond

IV of Toulouse illustrate the hazards of crusader travel. At age fifty-five, Raymond was considered elderly for the era. His main motivation for organizing a crusade was his wish to die in the Holy Land. In the winter of 1096–1097, the count set off for the East with his wife, an infant son, several hundred knights, and an equal number of unarmed peasants. The count was also joined by Raymond d'Aguiliers, a chaplain and chronicler who wrote about the journey.

Count Raymond's group chose to travel through the mountainous terrain of Slavonia in present-day Croatia. This turned out to be an unwise choice, as d'Aguiliers explains: "Slavonia was such a desert and so pathless and mountainous that we saw in it neither wild animals, nor birds for three weeks. The inhabitants of the region were so boorish and rude that they were unwilling to trade with us, or to furnish us guidance, but instead fled from their villages and their castles [upon our approach]."[16]

Bandits followed behind the count's party and preyed on the weak and old who fell behind. The knights, already sapped by hunger and thirst, had to fight at the rear to defend the peasants. Slavonian bandits who were captured were dealt with harshly. According to d'Aguiliers, the count "ordered the eyes of some of them (the prisoners) to be torn out, the feet of others cut off, and the nose and hands of still others to be slashed."[17]

After suffering a bruising journey for forty days, Raymond met with the king of Slavonia. The count paid the king a monetary tribute in exchange for food and supplies. However, the king did not honor the deal, and no goods were ever delivered. With no food, the hungry crusaders experienced trouble in nearly every town and village. Residents of the small town of Ruše attacked the group, and the count retaliated. His knights destroyed the city's walls, forced its citizens to surrender, and seized what d'Aguiliers describes as "great plunder."[18] The plunder probably included clothes, money, jewelry, pack animals, and any other items of value they could carry.

WORDS IN CONTEXT

pottage
A thick stew that was the staple food of medieval peasants, made from a random assortment of boiled vegetables, grains, and whatever meat or fish was available.

Deserted, Waterless Anatolia

There is little doubt that Raymond's forces stripped Ruše of its wine, beer, bread, meat, cheese, vegetables, and other foods. Finding nutrition was the main concern of all crusaders, who mostly survived on a thick stew called pottage made from boiled vegetables, grain, and whatever meat or fish was available.

Stealing food was a necessity; there were no restaurants or food stores. Most peasants struggled to survive on what little food was available and had little to sell. When a crusader army passed through a region, its troops might consume all of the food peasants stored for survival throughout the year. Little wonder that the hungry people of Slavonia were unhappy when the count and his followers passed through their territory on the way to Jerusalem in 1099.

The nutritional demands of crusaders—and their horses and pack animals—were enormous. Modern historians have determined that a large group of five thousand crusaders required more than 75,000 pounds (34,020 kg) of provisions for each week of operations. This was equal to the entire annual wheat output of a typical small village.

Feeding the troops and quenching their thirst became ever more difficult as crusaders marched out of the fertile lands of Europe and into the Eastern deserts. The arid highlands of Anatolia receive only about 12 inches (30.5 cm) of rain annually, about the same amount as the state of Arizona. Food and water shortages in this region made the crusaders vulnerable in the sparsely populated Anatolia, which was controlled by fierce Seljuk Turks.

When the crusader army led by the Italian Bohemond of Taranto crossed into central Anatolia in July 1097, the group faced immense difficulties. As described by the anonymous writer of the twelfth-century memoir called *Gesta Francorum* (*The Deeds of the Franks*): "[The land] was deserted, waterless, and uninhabitable, from which we barely emerged or escaped alive, for we suffered greatly from hunger and thirst, and found nothing at all to eat except prickly plants which we gathered and rubbed between our hands."[19]

In Their Own Words

Terror Tactics of Tramps

The eleventh-century chronicler Guibert of Nogent describes how fears of cannibalism were used as a terror tactic by an informal group of Christian fighters labeled Tarfurs, or tramps, by the Turks:

> There was a certain man of Norman birth, and of not low station in life, so they say, who started as a knight but became a foot-soldier; he saw that these men were wandering about without a lord, so he laid down his weapons and clothes, and volunteered to be their king. From then on he was called King Tarfur. For these men were called Tarfur [tramps] by the infidels [Turks]. . . . They are so called because they tramp, that is, they do things in a carefree way, traveling hither and thither throughout the years. . . .
>
> A hideous rumor spread among the infidel: that there were men in the Frankish army who fed very greedily on the bodies of Saracens. When they heard this the Tarfurs, in order to impress the enemy, roasted the bruised body of a Turk over a fire as if it were meat for eating, in full view of the Turkish forces.

Quoted in Elizabeth Hallam, ed., *Chronicles of the Crusades*. New York: Welcome Rain, 2000, p. 85.

Starving Martyrs

When the crusaders reached the Anatolian city of Nicaea, the local populace was all too willing to feed the famished Christians—for a price. Fulcher recalled that back home in Normandy, a live cow with her calf sold for the sum of four shillings. However, food sellers in Nicaea demanded two shillings for a single egg. A live chicken sold for nine shillings.

Although knights and nobles could afford expensive eggs, impoverished peasants could not; they ate rats and dogs. Others took to the barren fields, where they dug with their hands in search of grains of wheat, beans, or edible roots. Some tried to eat thistles, which caused severe irritation of the tongue and mouth. The eleventh-century chronicler Guibert of Nogent captures the scene: "[The] poorest people in the crusading army always marched barefoot, bore no arms, themselves had absolutely no money; but, entirely filthy in their nakedness and want . . . lived on roots of plants."[20]

In the winter of 1098, a continuous rain added to the crusaders' misery when their waterlogged canvas tents rotted and dissolved. As the French archbishop Anselm of Ribemont grimly describes it, "God, who chasteneth every son whom he loveth, so chastened us that . . . from lack of horses, or food, or through excessive cold, almost all were dying."[21]

> **WORDS IN CONTEXT**
> **shilling**
> A coin used during the medieval era, originally said to equal the value of a live cow or sheep.

Although accurate estimates of fatalities are difficult to find, at least five hundred crusaders died of starvation that winter. But Fulcher, who made the best of the bad situation, describes the victims as martyrs: "I believe the elect were tried by the Lord and by such suffering were cleansed of their sins. . . . [Many] of the people suffered long agony and gladly ran the full course of martyrdom. When they struggled against the pagans they labored for God."[22]

Crusader Cannibals

Although starved martyrs were lauded, the terrible hunger created desperation that led to ghastly behavior. Knights survived by sucking blood

Starvation and desperation led to ghastly behavior during the siege of Antioch (pictured). In some instances, knights cut their horses and sucked the blood from the wounds while others resorted to cannibalism.

from wounds made in their horses. People searched through piles of animal dung for undigested seeds and grain. In some places starvation was so widespread that a few resorted to cannibalism. This occurred during the first siege of the Crusades, when the crusader army got bogged down while trying to capture the Syrian city of Antioch.

The siege of Antioch lasted from late October 1097 until early June 1098 and turned into a starving contest. For more than seven months, the food stockpiled by Muslims within Antioch dwindled as they held off the foodless Christians camped outside the city's walls. Hundreds of starving crusaders deserted during this period, but some were driven to cannibalism. Fulcher describes the scene at the siege in the winter of 1098: "I shudder to say that many of our men, terribly tormented by the madness of starvation, cut pieces of flesh from the buttocks of Saracens lying there dead. These pieces they cooked and ate, savagely devouring the flesh while it was insufficiently roasted."[23]

During the long winter, an estimated one in five crusaders died of starvation. They eventually managed to take Antioch, but there was little food left in the city. Muslims in the surrounding countryside refused to sell food to the Christians, who continued to starve for months.

In later years reports of cannibal crusaders continued. In 1107 chronicler Ralph of Caen described Christians roasting children on spits. While some historians doubt the accuracy of this account, cannibalism stories were used as a way to terrorize the enemy. A group of crusaders who were called Tarfurs, or tramps, by the Turks took advantage of these fears. The Tarfurs roasted the body of a prisoner in full view of witnesses. They did not eat the flesh, but the act itself struck fear into the local populace.

Parched Tongues

While brutal acts of cannibalism were rare, water shortages were a constant problem for crusaders. And intense thirst was known to push Christians into madness. This was the case when the survivors of Raymond's army reached their final goal, the city of Jerusalem in June 1099. The city's Muslim governor, Iftikhar ad-Daulah, had poisoned the wells outside Jerusalem's city walls. This left only one pool of water about 6 miles (9.7 km) away. When the thirsty crusaders discovered the water, a riot broke out. As d'Aguiliers writes:

> [The water] was consumed with such great crowding and haste
> that the men pushed one another into it, and many baggage ani-

Looking Back

Tarantulas and Crocodiles

European crusaders were unfamiliar with the wide variety of spiders, scorpions, and other deadly creatures found in the East. Medieval history professor Ronald C. Finucane describes how King Richard I's troops dealt with these dangers during the Third Crusade, which began in 1189:

> After King Richard's men bedded down at night at a certain camp site, they were attacked by "swarms of tarantulas and stinging worms [scorpions]." It was found that one way to drive them off was to raise a tremendous din by beating on helmets, saddles, tubs, pots and kettles, shields and basins. Whenever these swarms were seen creeping up, the Crusaders leapt to their noisemakers. In another part of the Holy Land, Richard's people were harassed by flying insects that attacked the face and throat, causing swellings and disfigurements. As a result, for this part of the march they covered their faces with cloths. . . . But perhaps most unusual deaths not caused by enemy action on the Third Crusade involved two people who decided to bathe in a river near the camp. They were, so it was reported, eaten by crocodiles.

Ronald C. Finucane, *Soldiers of the Faith*. New York: St. Martin's, 1983, p. 66.

mals and cattle perished in it. And so when the pool was filled with the crowd and with the bodies of dead animals, the stronger, even at the price of death, forced their way to the very opening in the rocks through which the water flowed, while the weak got only the water which had already been contaminated. Many sick people fell down by the fountain, with tongues so parched that they were un-able to utter a word; with open mouths they stretched forth their hands toward those who had water.[24]

The fields surrounding the pool filled up with dead horses, mules, cattle, and sheep that died of thirst. When the animals rotted in the field, "there was a most sickening stench throughout the camp,"[25] according to d'Aguiliers. As the heat and dust increased the thirst of the mob, stronger members of the group combed the countryside in search of water. This was brought back to camp and sold to the highest bidder, although much of the water was murky and contaminated. Wine was a luxury that was barely mentioned. D'Aguiliers criticized the crusaders for putting their own needs before their duty to fight the Saracens: "[Few] were mindful of the Lord, or of such work as was needed to capture the city; nor did they take heed to beseech the Lord's favor. And thus we did not recognize God in the midst of our affliction, nor did He show favor to the ungrateful."[26]

Pitiful Cries of the Sick

Without proper food and clean water, crusaders were vulnerable to nu-merous diseases, which killed nearly as many soldiers as did the enemy. In 1097, when the army at Antioch camped near marshy ground, many crusaders were stricken with malaria spread by mosquitoes. They suffered headaches, fever, vomiting, convulsions, and death.

Dysentery, another common ailment among medieval soldiers, was called siege sickness. The disease swept through camps where sieges made it impossible for people to leave and find potable water. Dysentery is caused by water contaminated by feces, corpses, and other rotting material and causes severe fever, stomach pain, cramps, and diarrhea. A twelfth-century Muslim historian, Ibn al-Qalanisi, writes that dysentery is "a disease to be feared and one from which its victim scarcely recovers."[27]

Malnutrition, which leads to a severe lack of vitamin C, could result in scurvy. This gruesome disease that often struck sailors causes limbs to swell, gums to rot with gangrene, and teeth to fall out. Jean de Joinville, a chronicler of the Seventh Crusade, describes the army barber using his

Mourners attend the funeral of Godfrey of Bouillon, a knight and one of the leaders of the First Crusade. Many unfortunate souls, including Godfrey, died of the plague during the Crusades.

sheers to cut away the gangrenous gums of suffering soldiers: "It was pitiful to hear around the camp the cries of those whose dead flesh was being cut away; it was just like the cry of a woman in labor."[28]

The bubonic plague was another fearful disease common during the Crusades. The contagious disease, spread by fleas carried on rats, causes lymph nodes to swell for days until they burst. The pain is horrific. During the First Crusade, Godfrey of Bouillon was killed by the plague in Jerusalem. Around 1192, during the Third Crusade, the plague wiped out most of the army led by German emperor Frederick Barbarossa.

In addition to epidemics, accidents and battle were causes of injury to crusaders. And no one expected much in the way of medical help. There were few doctors, and Frankish medical treatments were ineffectual or, more often, deadly. Disease was viewed as a punishment from God, and a sick soldier often called a priest rather than a doctor. The Arab chronicler Usama describes a case in which a woman was treated for a high fever, which brought on hallucinations and hysteria. The Frankish physician believed she was possessed by the devil. He shaved her head, cut the flesh off the top of her skull, and rubbed salt into the wound while performing an exorcism meant to drive the devil out of her body. The woman soon died.

In one of the ironies of the Crusades, Franks who became ill often turned to Arab and Jewish doctors, who had medical skills far superior to the Europeans. Eastern doctors practiced medicine based on thousands of years of collective study dating back to ancient Egypt. In Jerusalem, Damascus, and other Eastern cities, Arab hospitals were large and well organized. In 1160 the archbishop William of Tyre wrote that sick and injured Franks, "urged by their womenfolk, scorned [Frankish] medicine and only trusted the Jews . . . Syrians, and Saracens."[29]

Joinville was among the Franks who benefited from Arab medicine, even when he was a prisoner of war. When he was captured by Muslims, his throat was so blocked he could not swallow. Joinville thought he had a tumor and assumed he was going to die. As the cousin of a Frankish king, Joinville's captors wished to keep him alive so they could trade him for a ransom. A Muslim doctor gave Joinville a liquid that cured him within two days.

Army Life

War has been described as hours of boredom mixed with moments of terror, and this expression accurately describes crusader war. While chroniclers like Joinville left detailed records of sickness, hunger, and other disasters, most of the time the crusaders lived like typical soldiers. Fighters kept boredom at bay drinking, joking, and betting on dice games.

Sometimes the term *playing dice* was a euphemism for another common activity, visiting a prostitute. According to medieval history professor James A. Brundage, "Armies of warriors under vows during the First Crusade were overrun by harlots . . . [and] brothels were clearly a normal component of the Crusaders' camps."[30] Leaders periodically attempted to expel prostitutes from their camps, but this was only a temporary solution; the women soon returned.

Most of the time, crusaders spent their days mending their clothes, sharpening their swords, repairing their equipment, and talking with friends. People prayed, gossiped about their leaders, and argued about politics. And almost all were homesick, struck by the sweet memories of their native lands and those they left behind.

Despite insects, disease, hunger, thirst, muddy roads, and hostile bandits, numerous people made it all the way to the Holy Land. Driven by deep religious beliefs and the promise of riches, the crusaders believed God was on their side. Whether they lived or died, the promise of eternal life was all but assured.

Chapter Three

Crusaders Battle for Jerusalem

On June 7, 1099, the Christian army approached the stone walls of Jerusalem under the searing desert sun. The Christians of the First Crusade had survived a three-year journey marked by starvation, thirst, disease, and bloodshed. Of the 10,000 knights who left Europe in 1096, only about 1,300 lived to see Jerusalem. Of the 45,000 original foot soldiers, about 15,000 survived. As they gathered near the city most sacred to Christianity, the crusaders were overcome with emotion. Twelfth-century French historian Albert of Aix (also known as Albert of Aachen) describes the scene: "All the people burst into floods of happy tears, because they were so close to the holy place of that longed-for city, for which they had suffered so many hardships, so many dangers, so many kinds of death and famine."[31]

But it would take more than happiness and religious fervor to conquer Jerusalem. The city was not large—about 212 acres (86 ha), or 130 city blocks. But Jerusalem was the most heavily fortified city in the medieval world. It was surrounded by a stone wall 50 feet (15.2 m) high and 10 feet (3 m) thick. This was reinforced by a secondary outer wall, called a curtain wall. The entire structure was surrounded by a deep, dry ditch called a moat.

Residents entered and left the city through five gates built into the walls, each defended from a pair of tall towers. Above the entire city, the Tower of David rose 145 feet (44 m) into the air. Built in the second century BCE, the Tower of David was a citadel, the last line of defense should an enemy breach the city's walls. It was strengthened by Muslims after they conquered Jerusalem in 638 to prevent Christians from retaking the city. In 1099 the tower was supplied with enough arms, food, water, and other resources to withstand an extended siege. As Fulcher of Chartres noted, "The Tower of David is of solid masonry half-way up, of large square blocks sealed with molten lead. Fifteen or twenty men, if well supplied with food, could defend it from all assaults of an enemy."[32]

Scaling the Wall

Jerusalem was ruled by a Muslim governing body called the Fatimid Caliphate, which also ruled Egypt and much of northern Africa. Inside the city walls, the Fatimid governor Iftikhar ad-Daulah commanded several thousand troops, including four hundred elite Egyptian cavalrymen. Frankish knights could enter the city using only one method. They would have to build scaling ladders, climb the walls, and fight the city's defenders in hand-to-hand combat.

The crusaders were stopped in their tracks by what seemed like an insurmountable problem. The desert land around Jerusalem was barren; there were no trees to make ladders. However, a young French marquis named Tancred discovered a solution by chance. Stricken with dysentery, Tancred went searching for an isolated cave where he could relieve himself. He eventually found

WORDS IN CONTEXT

moat

A wide, deep ditch, either filled with water or dry, used as a line of defense around a castle, fort, or city.

such a cave. The chaplain and crusade chronicler Ralph of Caen picks up the story: "After relieving himself and gaining back his strength, he noticed four pieces of wood on the opposite wall of the cave. One could not hope for anything more useful for the task at hand. When he saw them, so great was his joy, that he could not believe it or trust his eyes. He got up and went over to touch them and see them more closely."[33]

Tancred's discovery was seen as a divine miracle by crusaders. The wood was used to build a large scaling ladder. On June 13 the ladder was slid over the curtain wall and propped up against the main wall of Jerusalem. The first man up was the French knight Raimbold Creton. However, when he reached up and grabbed the top of the wall, his hand was promptly chopped off by an enemy sword. Others followed, as described

The Tower of David (pictured) rises high over the city of Jerusalem. The citadel provided a last line of defense against enemies who managed to breach city walls.

in the *Gesta Francorum*: "Against the great wall we set up one ladder, up which our knights climbed and fought hand to hand with the Saracens with swords and spears. We lost many men but the enemy lost more."[34]

Despite killing many Fatimids, the crusaders failed in their first attempt to take Jerusalem. They returned to their camps to organize a siege.

Everyone United

Frankish knights were skilled at charging into battle on horseback, wielding lances and swords. But a siege was a key element of crusader combat. Those executing the siege—and those under siege—spent weeks staring at one another while waiting for the other side to exhaust its food and water supplies.

During the siege of Jerusalem, food remained plentiful among the

Franks. However, water was in short supply, as the *Gesta Francorum* explains: "We were so oppressed by thirst that we sewed together the hides of oxen and buffalo, which we used to carry water over a distance of about six miles. Because of the vile-smelling water from these vessels . . . we were in daily distress and affliction."[35]

With the Fatimids trapped in the city, the Franks had time to build what were called siege engines. These weapons of war included catapults, battering rams, and towers for scaling fortified walls. Obtaining wood for siege engines would have been impossible if not for the unwitting actions of Jerusalem's governor ad-Daulah.

In preparation for the siege, ad-Daulah evicted Jerusalem's Christians, fearing they might work within the city to sabotage Fatimid defense efforts. The homeless Christians joined the Frankish besiegers and showed them where wood could be found in the local forests. Within hours bundles of timber were being transported to Frankish camps, tied to the backs of camels.

Over the course of the next three weeks, the crusaders worked with frantic energy to build siege engines. According to d'Aguiliers: "Everyone united to further the task, by labor, by construction and by generally helping. No one was lazy and no one slacked. Everyone worked voluntarily, except for the craftsmen, who were paid from a collection taken from among the people."[36]

> **WORDS IN CONTEXT**
>
> **mangonel**
>
> From the Latin for "engine of war," a catapult weapon used to hurl objects such as rocks and flaming tar from a bowl-shaped bucket.

Building Siege Engines

The workers constructed three massive siege towers. Two of the towers rose to about 30 feet (9 m) and one was more than 52 feet (16 m) tall. Each tower contained several horizontal platforms where soldiers could stand and launch arrows. The entire tower framework was covered by protective walls constructed from wattle covered by animal hides. These barriers shielded both the tower and the soldiers. The towers were affixed to huge, wheeled platforms that could be rolled up against the city walls.

The crusaders also assembled numerous other siege engines. Battering rams were fashioned from massive tree trunks. Large iron plates were attached to the ends. Each battering ram was mounted on a wheeled platform and protected by a wattle roof. These would be used to bang down the massive wooden city gates of Jerusalem.

Catapults called mangonels were perhaps the most formidable siege engines. Each mangonel had a bowl-shaped bucket at the end of a long arm that shot forward when fired. The mangonel could hurl projectiles such as heavy stones or casks of burning tar for distances of 1,300 feet (396 m). As a weapon of intimidation, the mangonel could be used to fling fresh animal dung, diseased corpses, or even human heads into enemy encampments.

Crusaders prepare for the assault on Jerusalem. Preparations included the construction of siege engines and siege towers.

Before any siege engine could be moved into place, however, the dry moat surrounding Jerusalem had to be crossed. This required a special effort, as Albert of Aix explains: "Our leaders discussed how they should fill in the ditch, and they had it announced that if anyone would bring three stones to cast into that pit, he should have a penny. It took three days and nights to fill it."[37]

Intimidating the Enemy

As the Franks worked to invade Jerusalem, ad-Daulah 's men made their own preparations. They wheeled their mangonels into place and piled up sacks of sand and straw to fortify the city gates. These were secured with very thick ropes normally used on ships.

Tensions mounted as the Franks worked to intimidate their enemies. In one incident an elderly Muslim noble was kidnapped outside the city walls by the French knight Baldwin of Bourcq. The Franks were impressed with the wisdom and dignity of the Fatimid nobleman and repeatedly tried to convert him to Christianity. Albert describes what happened when the prisoner refused: "He was brought out in front of the Tower of David to frighten the guards of the citadel and was beheaded by Baldwin's squire in full view of all."[38]

In another instance the Franks captured a Fatimid spy. After interrogating the man, the Franks loaded the spy—still alive—into a mangonel and tried to launch him back into Jerusalem. The man was too heavy, however, and he only flew as far as the sharp stones piled up around the city walls. These broke his neck, shattered his bones, and killed him instantly.

The Fatimids had their own methods for angering the enemy, as Albert writes, "To arouse the [Franks'] anger, they fixed crosses on top of the walls in mockery and abuse, upon which they either spat, or they did not shrink from urinating on them in full view of everyone."[39]

When siege preparations were near completion, the crusaders participated in a ritual meant to unite them in their cause while simultaneously cleansing them of their sins. On July 8, 1099, Frankish clergymen assembled with crosses and relics (physical remains and personal effects of

In Their Own Words

Arrows "Fell like Hail"

When the crusaders rolled their siege towers next to Jerusalem's main walls, the Fatimid defenders responded with a massive barrage of stones, arrows, and firebrands, as Raymond d'Aguiliers writes:

> From every side stones were hurled . . . and so many arrows that they fell like hail. The servants of [God] bore this patiently, sustained by the premises of their faith, whether they should be killed or should presently prevail over their enemies. The battle showed no indication of victory, but when the [siege towers] were drawn nearer to the walls, they hurled not only stones and arrows, but also burning wood and straw. The wood was dipped in pitch, wax, and sulfur; then straw and tow [flax] were fastened on by an iron band, and, when lighted, these firebrands were shot from [mangonels]. They were all bound together by an iron band, I say, so that wherever they fell, the whole mass held together and continued to burn. Such missiles, burning as they shot upward, could not be resisted by swords or by high walls; it was not even possible for the defenders to find safety down behind the walls. Thus the fight continued from the rising to the setting sun in such splendid fashion that it is difficult to believe anything more glorious was ever done.

Raymond d'Aguiliers, "Historia francorum qui ceperint Jerusalem," Internet Medieval Sourcebook, Fordham University, December 1997. www.fordham.edu.

saints). The Franks formed a procession with knights, foot soldiers, and peasants. All were barefoot as they blew horns and brandished arms. The Franks marched to the Mount of Olives, a ridge adjacent to Jerusalem where Christians believe Jesus ascended to heaven after the Resurrection.

The Fatimids viewed the procession as a chance to harass their enemies. When the Franks later passed close to Jerusalem's walls, they were peppered with arrows. Dozens were wounded.

Dressing for Battle

On July 14 the day dawned hot and dry as the Frankish trumpets blew, alerting crusaders that the long-anticipated attack on Jerusalem was about to begin. The knights and foot soldiers pulled on their hauberks, knee-length protective mesh armor called mail. Each hauberk was made from about thirty thousand small, interlinked iron rings and weighed at least 22 pounds (10 kg). The hauberk covered a knight's body, forearms, wrists, and hands. Mail leggings protected the legs and feet, and scarf-like armor called a coif was draped around the head and neck.

A Christian soldier also wore combat headgear with a conical top known as the Norman helmet. This helmet sat on the head like a hat and did not protect the eyes or mouth. Full facial helmets with small openings for the eyes were not used until the thirteenth century. However, the Norman helmet, also called the nasal helmet, featured a metal bar that extended from the rim to protect the wearer's nose.

An iron helmet and hauberk made for an extremely hot fighting uniform. As Albert writes, on the day of the assault, "the Christian army was severely tormented by the heat of the blazing sun and by the unbearable lack of water and the incredibly arid landscape."[40]

While heat and weight made fighting in armor more difficult, the attire offered surprisingly effective protection from slashing swords and Saracen arrows. There were stories of men returning to camp unharmed after battle with dozens of arrows sticking out of their mail.

Surprise Attack

Jerusalem's Fatimid defenders were prepared for a fight, but they were unprepared for the surprise attack planned by the Frankish leader Godfrey of Bouillon. For three weeks the Franks had been building a massive siege tower beyond the range of Fatimid arrows near Jerusalem's northern wall, in view of the Tower of David. The Fatimids assumed the Franks would begin their attack from this location. They added extra fortifications to the walls and concentrated their troops there. But the siege tower was experimental and unlike any built before; it could be broken down into portable sections and reassembled where it was needed. In the dark of night, before the battle began, the tower was secretly moved and rebuilt in a lightly defended spot outside St. Stephen's Gate (now called Lions' Gate). As Fulcher explains: "When the command was given, they transported the tower, in sections, by night to a corner of the city. In the morning, they quickly erected it, assembled, not far from the wall . . . and well protected on the outside with hides, they pushed it little by little nearer the wall."[41]

The Franks also rolled their mangonels to the curtain wall outside St. Stephen's Gate in the middle of the night. When the sun rose, the battle cry went up as the crusaders began efforts to break through Jerusalem's outer wall to reach the main walls of the city. Frankish catapults pounded the curtain wall with barrage after barrage of heavy stones. This withering attack prevented the Fatimid defenders from mounting an effective counterattack.

Away from the mangonels, a battering ram was wheeled into place. As the sun rose in the sky, the crusaders pounded away at the curtain wall, creating a large opening. The Franks were then able to wheel the battering ram up to the city's much stronger main wall.

Flaming Firebrands

When the Franks approached Jerusalem's wall, the Fatimids rained fire on them with flaming missiles called firebrands. These were made of wooden mallets wrapped in straw and doused in a flammable mixture of wax, sulfur, and plant resin called pitch. The mallets were studded with sharp nails protruding from the heads. When launched from mangonels, the firebrands stuck to whatever wood or flesh they hit. These deadly weapons burned to death hundreds of Franks.

The firebrands also set the battering ram on fire, creating a unique problem. The flaming battering ram blocked the breach in the wall and prevented the Franks from rolling their siege tower up to the city's main wall. Eventually, the battering ram burned to cinders while the sun set. The battle for Jerusalem was over for now; without modern lighting, medieval battles stopped at dusk. However, few people rested, as d'Aguiliers writes:

> Night brought fear to both sides. The Saracens feared that we would take the city . . . the next day, for the outer works were broken through and the ditch was filled, so that it was possible to make an entrance through the wall very quickly. On our part, we feared only that the Saracens would set fire to the machines that were moved so close to the walls, and thus improve their situation. So on both sides it was a night of watchfulness, labor, and sleepless caution. . . . It is hard to believe how great were the efforts made on both sides during the night.[42]

A Bloody Victory

At dawn the next morning Godfrey affixed a large golden cross to the tallest siege tower. Just as the Fatimids feared, dozens of fighters climbed aboard and the tower was inched through the breach in the curtain wall. Godfrey himself occupied the top platform. Mangonels from both sides launched frenzied barrages of firebrands and stones, shattering skulls, breaking bones, and searing the flesh of countless fighters. One man standing directly next to Godfrey had his neck snapped by an enemy stone. However, the wattle screens protected the tower as the Fatimid firebrands slid off the slippery animal hides.

In desperation two Fatimid women tried to stop the advancing Franks by casting a curse on a mangonel. As d'Aguiliers writes, the women "tried to bewitch one of the hurling machines, but a stone struck and crushed them . . . so that their lives were extinguished and the evil incantations averted."[43]

The wall at St. Stephen's Gate was about 46 feet (14 m) tall, which gave Godfrey's siege tower a 6-foot (2 m) height advantage over the

Muslims, Jews, Africans, and others fled the Frankish army, seeking refuge in Solomon's Temple (pictured in the center of this map of the ancient city of Jerusalem). Rather than finding safety, they were slaughtered by the thousands.

defenders. The tower was moved into position about 3 feet (1 m) from Jerusalem's main wall. Frankish soldiers shot arrows from crossbows and stones from slingshots.

The desperate Fatimids responded with their most destructive weapon, commonly known as Greek fire. This mixture of incendiary chemicals such as tar, quicklime, sulfur, and saltpeter could not be extinguished with water. However, the Christians evicted by the governor proved to be helpful once again. They had previously warned the Franks about Greek fire and instructed them to douse the flames with vinegar. Forewarned, Godfrey's men stocked the tower with leather bags filled with vinegar. When the Greek fire was launched, the flames were immediately put out.

As the sun rose high in the sky, the battle turned in the Frank's favor, due to their abundant use of fire. The crusaders managed to place scaling ladders against the walls; from these ladders they launched flaming arrows wrapped in burning cotton at a wooden defense tower. The tower caught fire, which spread flames to the wooden substructure of the main wall.

The fire drove the Fatimids away, and Godfrey took advantage of the situation. He cut one of the hide-covered wattles from the siege tower and used it as a temporary bridge to the main wall. A mob of crusaders, led by Godfrey, stormed over the makeshift bridge while dozens more climbed the walls on scaling ladders. The Fatimid defenses quickly collapsed. D'Aguiliers provides an eyewitness account to the bloody aftermath:

> Now that our men had possession of the walls and [Fatimid defense] towers, wonderful sights were to be seen. Some of our men (and this was more merciful) cut off the heads of their enemies; others shot them with arrows, so that they fell from the towers; others tortured them longer by casting them into the flames. Piles of heads, hands, and feet were to be seen in the streets of the city. It was necessary to pick one's way over the bodies of men and horses.[44]

Unholy Brutality

Although the battle was over, the bloodshed continued as the Frankish army sacked Jerusalem in a horrific rampage. As Thomas Asbridge writes, "In the long-imagined moment of victory, with their pious ambitions realized, they unleashed an unholy wave of brutality throughout the city, surpassing all that had gone before."[45]

Many of Jerusalem's Muslims, Jews, Africans, and other non-Christians fled to Solomon's Temple. Fulcher claims ten thousand people were beheaded there and the temple ran ankle deep in blood. Elsewhere in Jerusalem, men, women, and children were slain without pity. As Albert describes it, "they were beheading or striking down with stones girls, women, noble ladies, even pregnant women, and very young children, paying attention to no one's age. . . . [Not] a suckling male child or female, not even an infant of one year would escape alive the hand of the murderer."[46]

WORDS IN CONTEXT
Resurrection
The rising again of Jesus Christ three days after his death.

Looking Back

The City of Jerusalem

Thomas Asbridge, a London professor of medieval history, describes the rich religious history of Jerusalem:

> Of all the cities encountered by the First Crusaders, none could exceed the historic and spiritual resonance of Jerusalem. Across 3,000 years of human settlement, the passing of countless generations, the city became inseparably entwined with the genesis and essence of three religions. This was the epicenter of Christianity, the site of Jesus' Passion. It was also the seat of the Israelites—the first city of Judaism—and the third holiest city in the Islamic world, deeply revered as the site of Mohammed's ascent to heaven. Jerusalem's spiritual stature was matched by its imposing physical presence. . . .
>
> Within its walls lay a prize beyond measure: the Church Of The Holy Sepulchre. It was to liberate this, the most sacred site on earth—where Christ had died on the cross then arisen reborn—that they left their homes in Europe and faced the horrors of the journey east.

Thomas Asbridge, *The First Crusade*. Oxford: Oxford University Press, 2004, pp. 299–300.

When not murdering Jerusalem's citizens, the Franks pillaged its wealth. An anonymous witness wrote in the *Gesta Francorum*, "Our men rushed around the whole city, seizing gold and silver, horses and mules, and houses full of all sorts of goods."[47] The plundering took a more ghastly turn when the crusaders realized that some citizens had swallowed their gold coins in a desperate effort to save them. According to Fulcher, "Our squires and poorer footmen discovered a trick of the Saracens, for they learned that they could find *byzants* [gold coins] in the stomachs and intestines of the dead Saracens, who had swallowed them. Thus, after several days they burned a great heap of dead bodies, that they might more easily get the precious metal from the ashes."[48]

After weeks of siege, warfare, murder, and plunder, the Franks finally gathered to worship. As Asbridge writes, "In a moment that is perhaps the most vivid distillation of the crusading experience, they came, still covered in their enemy's blood, weighed down with booty, rejoicing and weeping from excessive gladness to worship at the [Church of the Holy] Sepulcher."[49]

Against the odds, the survivors of the three-year march to Jerusalem had succeeded in their goal. The city was now claimed by Christians, just as Urban had commanded in 1096. As sorrow and despair cut through Jerusalem's Muslim and Jewish quarters, a wave of resounding joy quickly spread to France, Italy, and Germany and throughout the Christian West.

Chapter Four

Saladin's Army Defeats the Crusaders

After Christian crusaders successfully used siege warfare to capture Jerusalem in 1099, they set up crusader kingdoms throughout the Holy Land. The kingdom of Jerusalem stretched from Beirut in modern Lebanon to Gaza in southwestern Israel.

The crusader lords imposed a feudal society on the multicultural, capitalist Arab culture. The crusader knight Baldwin I was made the Latin king of Jerusalem. He named European counts to rule Tripoli and Edessa as semi-independent kingdoms. These crusader lords were obliged to render military service to Baldwin and abide by his judgments and rulings. Large tracts of land and castles were handed out to Franks, who ran their lordships as feudal estates.

During the years of the crusader kingdoms, the Franks repressed and murdered Muslims, Jews, and other non-Christians living under their rule. However, during much of that time, Muslims lacked the means to effectively fight back against the crusaders.

Throughout most of the twelfth century, no single Muslim leader had a large standing army. The Arab world was divided between regional warlords who battled one another to gain control over local territories. The situation changed in 1174 when a military officer known as Saladin became the sultan, or supreme ruler, of Egypt and Damascus.

A Formidable Force

After becoming sultan, Saladin and his large extended family, the Ayyubids, united a huge portion of the Middle East through war and diplomacy. By 1185 Saladin controlled most of Syria, Egypt, Iraq, and Turkey, regions that were rich in military manpower. In the spring of 1187, Saladin used this manpower to mobilize one of the largest Muslim armies the medieval world had ever seen. The army, assembled south of Damascus, grew to include twelve thousand professional cavalrymen and thirty thousand volunteer soldiers.

Throughout May and June Saladin trained his troops to perform a series of complex battle maneuvers. When the troops drilled, they raised a cloud of dust so thick that Saladin said it "darkened the eye of the sun."[50]

The army was divided into three formidable contingents, with a right flank, a left flank, and a central force under Saladin's personal command. The plan was to surround and destroy the army of Christian knights and foot soldiers who defended Jerusalem.

A Call to Jihad

Saladin was the first Muslim ruler to turn his full attention toward waging war against Christians. His decision to retake Jerusalem was driven by a quest for power and glory but also motivated by jihad of the sword. Saladin had been under pressure from religious scholars and Muslim refugees for more than a decade to wage a holy countercrusade.

The concept of waging jihad against Christians was initially put forth in 1105 by the Islamic scholar Ali ibn Tahir al-Sulami. As al-Sulami wrote in a treatise called *Kitab al-Jihad* (*Book of the Holy War*):

> **WORDS IN CONTEXT**
> **cistern**
> A large, waterproof receptacle built to store rainwater, usually underground.

> It is true and clear that the jihad against this group and their objective is incumbent on all who are capable and have no horrible illness or chronic malady, or blindness, or weakness from old age. As for those who are excluded from these, either rich or poor, having two parents, either owing a debt or owed a debt, they are obliged to go out to fight in this situation, and to set out to put an end to the fearful consequence of weakness and reticence.[51]

The Muslim leader and military commander Saladin presides over the surrender of a leading crusader knight. Saladin was the first Muslim ruler to turn his full attention toward war against the crusading Christians.

Al-Sulami died the following year, but his call to jihad resounded through the Muslim world for decades. In the middle of the twelfth century, Nur al-Din, the Seljuk Turkish ruler of Syria, renewed the call to holy war. Echoing al-Sulami, al-Din wrote that defensive jihad was the ethical duty of every able-bodied Muslim male.

Al-Din's treatise provided a detailed list of obligations for those entering defensive jihad. He wrote that any warrior still living with his parents should seek their permission before waging holy war. If married, the warrior should ensure that his wife and children would be cared for. Al-Din stated that a warrior on a battlefield should stand his ground unless he was threatened by two or more infidels. Warriors were warned not to kill women or children. Al-Din also stated that a jihadist should not accept payment for fighting. However, he believed religious warriors had a right to plunder the riches of the infidels.

Saladin's Slave Soldiers

Saladin had once been a staff officer under al-Din. When al-Din died in 1174, Saladin recruited soldiers he had served with as a core fighting force from which to build his army. And the soldiers of Saladin's new force came from many different backgrounds. The leadership was made up mostly of Turkish and Kurdish military professionals called emirs. Emirs were granted control of large tracts of land—and the taxes collected from it—in exchange for the promise of military service.

The emirs oversaw troops called Mamluks (sometimes spelled *mameluks*), who were Egyptian slaves. Mamluks were kidnapped as children and trained under strict military discipline for years. Most Mamluks did not know their real parents or their birth names. They were all called by a single name: Ibn Abdullah, or "son of Abdullah." This refers to Abdullah, father of Muhammad, the man who founded the Islamic faith in the seventh century. Because they were conditioned to be trustworthy and loyal, elite Mamluk fighters often acted as guards and advisers to sultans and other high officials.

The Mamluks were known for their ability to fight while mounted on swift horses, which they decorated with colorful ribbons. The Mamluks carried fearsome curved sabers that could slice off a man's arm with a single stroke.

"Swarms of Wasps"

Seljuk Turks were another formidable element of Saladin's army. They fought on horseback like Christian knights but traveled light. The Turks did not wear heavy mail but dressed in leather tunics that repelled arrows. Their compact conical helmets were inscribed with verses from the Koran.

The Turks were expert archers who wielded light, agile bows from

Looking Back

Training Mamluk Warriors

The Mamluks were slave warriors who were kidnapped as children. Robert Irwin, historian and scholar of Arabic literature, describes the Mamluks' rigorous military training exercises:

The young Mamluks in the Cairo citadel embarked on a punishing schedule of military training. They were made to slice at lumps of clay with their swords as many as 1,000 times a day so as to build up their arm muscles. They were taught bareback riding and horse archery, with special emphasis on how to fire backwards from the saddle. An important exercise was shooting up and back at a gourd raised on a high pole. The horse archer had to drop his reins to fire and guide the horse with his knees as he fired his arrow, and it was not unknown for tyro [beginner] Mamluks to die as they crashed into the pole. Fatalities were also common in polo, an aristocratic sport which doubled as training for warfare. Large-scale organized hunting expeditions had a similar function. . . .

Mamluks were also instructed in Arabic and Islam and quite a few learned to read and write. The formation of an educated military elite . . . explains the proliferation of treatises on *furusiyya. Furusiyya* literally means horsemanship, but works in this genre dealt not only with the management of horses, but with all the skills related to warfare, including use of the sword, bow, lance, and later cannon, as well as the deployment of siege engines and the conduct of armies.

Quoted in Jonathan Riley-Smith, ed., *The Oxford Illustrated History of the Crusades*. Oxford: Oxford University Press, 1995, p. 241.

the saddle, shooting arrows without slowing or dismounting. They defended themselves with round shields that were smaller and lighter than the heavy, kite-shape shields carried by the Franks. And while the Franks needed large, slow horses to carry their heavy arms and armor, Turkish horses were smaller, faster, and more nimble.

Crusading knights rode together in long lines, three or four abreast. This solid formation presented an easy target for the Turks, who used their superior mobility and light weapons to great advantage. When approaching the enemy, the Turks at first remained at a distance before swooping in for a lightning-fast attack. Writing in 1148, Princess Anna Comnena described a Turkish attack against a crusader army commanded by a general named Bryennius: "Forthwith, at a given signal, [the Turks] rode through them like swarms of wasps, from various directions, and with their loud war-cries, and shouts, and incessant shooting, not only filled the ears of Bryennius' men with a terrible din, but also utterly obscured their sight by showering arrows upon them from all sides."[52]

By buzzing back and forth like wasps, the Turks made difficult targets for sword-wielding Franks. If the Turks faced a charging group of knights, they retreated in every direction, only to veer their horses around and attack again. William of Tyre used a different type of insect to describe the Turkish fighters: "Now they faced the enemy, now they turned away; they thought it no less credible to retreat than to pursue; they were like flies who could be beaten off but not driven away."[53]

WORDS IN CONTEXT

emir

An Arabic word used in medieval times to designate someone who was a commander, general, or ruler.

The armor and shields worn by Christian knights protected them from enemy arrows. However, during this era, horses did not wear armor. The Turks destroyed the ability of knights to charge or retreat by shooting the horses out from under them. When the knights were forced to fight on foot, the Turks swung their bows over their backs and moved in on their targets with swinging clubs, swords, and sabers.

After Turks and Mamluks dominated the enemy from horseback, the infantry followed. These foot soldiers marched in columns wielding axes, spears, and crossbows. The Muslim infantry included Syrians, Egyptians, black Africans from the Sudan, and Bedouin nomads from the Middle East. Around 1185 an English priest named Richard de Templo described the Sudanese, the Bedouins, and their weapons: "Instead of wearing helmets, [the Africans] wore red coverings on their heads, brandishing in the hands clubs bristling with iron teeth, whose shattering blows neither helmets nor mailshirts could resist. . . . [The Bedouins are] the most redoubtable infantrymen, carrying bows and quivers and round shields. They are a very energetic and agile race."[54]

Inciting a War

While Saladin was uniting a powerful army, the Franks were fighting among themselves. During the 1180s the crusader kingdoms were on the verge of collapse as various factions struggled for control. To unite the warring Christian factions, the Frankish governor of Antioch, Raynald of Châtillon, devised what seemed to be an odd plan. He decided to provoke Saladin to start a war. Raynald hoped this would force the Franks to put aside their differences in order to defend the kingdom from the sultan.

In 1186 Raynald attacked a Muslim merchant caravan traveling between Cairo and Damascus. The wagons of the caravan were loaded with cloth, jewels, spices, and other treasures. Raynald kidnapped the merchants and their families and confiscated their riches. When Saladin learned of this affront, he sent envoys to Raynald to demand compensation. Raynald refused to return the booty. Several months later, Raynald attacked another caravan, this one carrying Saladin's sister. This prompted Saladin to declare war on the crusaders. The sultan swore he would capture and kill Raynald at any cost.

Armies Assemble for Battle

Many battles during the Crusades were sieges, but the battle between Saladin's forces and the Franks involved horsemen, infantrymen, and sword-wielding fighters on an open battlefield. The war began on July 2, 1187, when Saladin led an army of forty-two thousand across the River

Jordan to the town of Tiberias, located near the Sea of Galilee.

In addition to his regular army, Saladin's forces were joined by numerous *mutawwiun*, civilian volunteers dedicated to waging jihad. According to the anonymous Frankish text *The Capture of the Holy Land by Saladin*, Saladin "gathered together an army as numerous as the sands of the seashore in order to wage war."[55]

When the Frankish king of Jerusalem, Guy de Lusignan, learned that Saladin was approaching, he assembled an army that included twelve hundred knights and about eighteen thousand infantrymen. Not all were professional soldiers. Guy had called on every able-bodied Christian male to defend the kingdom of Jerusalem. *The Capture of the Holy Land by Saladin* describes the situation: "Not a man fit for war remained in the cities, towns, or castles without being urged to leave by the King's order. . . . [They] gave a fee to everyone who could bear a lance or bow into battle. . . . They gloried in their multitude of men, the trappings of their horses, in their breastplates, helmets, lances, and golden shields."[56]

> **WORDS IN CONTEXT**
> **dinar**
> A type of gold or silver coin used as currency in the Muslim world.

Trapped at the Horns of Hittin

On July 3 Guy's army rode out of Jerusalem, the summer sun beating down on iron helmets and mail. The weather was blazing hot, and Saladin understood that water would play a decisive role in the conflict. He ordered all the cisterns in the region emptied while leaving a single, heavily guarded spring to supply his troops.

Around noon, as Guy's large, armored legion crept forward, Saladin sent several divisions to circle behind the Franks, preventing any retreat. Meanwhile, the main contingent of his army was set up to block Guy's men from advancing on Tiberias.

Saladin wanted to attack the Franks on a desert plateau between two long hills, called the Horns of Hittin (sometimes spelled Hattin) outside Tiberias. Guy's army walked directly into the sultan's trap. As the sun set, the Franks pitched camp on the waterless, unprotected plateau, his men

Saladin set a trap for the Franks on a desert plateau between two hills known as the Horns of Hittin (shown here in more recent times). The Franks set up camp on the plateau, unaware that they were surrounded by Saladin's warriors.

weak and suffering from dire thirst. The troops were hemmed in by a wall of Muslim soldiers—according to William, "so close that they could talk to one another, and if a cat had fled from the Christian host it could not have escaped without the Saracens taking it."[57]

Observing the scene, Saladin's men felt festive, according to Arab chronicler Ali Ibn al-Athir:

> The Muslims for their part had lost their first fear of the enemy and were in high spirits, and spent the night inciting one another to battle. They could smell victory in the air, and the more they saw of the unexpectedly low morale of the Franks the more aggressive and daring they became; throughout the night the cries Allah akbar [God is great] and "there is no God but Allah" rose up to heaven.[58]

Smoke and Thirst

During the night, Saladin's men collected brush, dry grass, and sticks and made piles of flammable material around the Frankish camp. The next morning, fires were lit. According to William, "This was quickly done. The fires burned vigorously and made an enormous amount of smoke, and this, in addition to the heat of the sun, caused the Christians considerable discomfort and harm."[59] To further torment his enemy, Saladin brought in a caravan of water-bearing camels and placed jars of the precious liquid around the enemy encampment. As the dehydrated Christians watched, the jars were emptied onto the ground. Saladin later wrote that the smoke and thirst were "a reminder of what God has prepared for them in the next world."[60]

As the stifling smoke billowed through the Franks' camp, Saladin implemented another element of his war plan. The night before, the sultan had handed out thousands of arrows to his skilled archers. At a given signal around noon, the bombardment was launched. Arrows flew through the blinding smoke, showering down on the desperate, thirsty Franks. A knight named Raymond of Tripoli launched a charge at one Turkish contingent, but the horsemen simply scattered, diffusing the Frankish force. Another group of renowned knights escaped, leaving demoralized soldiers behind to face their deaths at the hands of the Muslim archers.

Dancing Lances

King Guy remained with about five hundred men; they climbed to a rocky saddle, a low point between the Horns of Hittin. The army retreated behind a wall still standing from an ancient fort that once occupied the saddle. The king managed to pitch his red royal tent as arrows rained down on his men.

Guy's only hope was to strike directly at Saladin and demoralize the Muslims by tearing down the sultan's yellow flag, which flew above the camp. Frankish horsemen launched a furious charge over the saddle and headed directly for the enemy fighters, but a Muslim counterattack drove them back up the hill. An Arab official named al-Afdal wrote that the Muslims' "pliant lances danced and were fed on [Christian] entrails [and their] sword blades sucked away their lives and scattered them on the hillsides."[61]

The Franks were defeated. They dismounted and sat down on the ground while the Muslims pulled down the king's tent. Thousands had been killed and thousands more were taken prisoner, including Guy and many nobles. As al-Athir describes it: "The number of dead and captured was so large that those who saw the slain could not believe that anyone could have been taken alive, and those who saw the prisoners could not believe that any had been killed. From the time of their first assault on Palestine in 1098 until now the Franks had never suffered such a defeat."[62]

Prisoners of War

When the battle subsided Saladin's personal secretary, Imad al-Din, described the scene of a battlefield where the dust was stained red with blood and littered with shattered corpses: "I passed by them and saw the limbs of the fallen cast naked on the field of combat, scattered in pieces over the site of the encounter, lacerated and disjointed, with heads cracked open, throats split, spines broken, necks shattered, feet in pieces, noses mutilated, extremities torn off, members dismembered, parts shredded."[63] Guy and Raynald of Châtillon were taken prisoner and brought to Saladin's large campaign tent. After waging such cunning and effective warfare, the sultan was charitable to Guy, whom he planned to hold for ransom in Damascus. Guy was shaking uncontrollably and dying of thirst. Saladin gave the Christian king of Jerusalem a golden chalice filled with cold water. According to Arab custom, offering a gift of food or water was equal to a promise of protection.

After drinking his fill, Guy moved to pass the cup to Raynald but was stopped by Saladin, who did not wish to offer protection to the man who had attacked his sister's caravan. Instead, the sultan scolded Raynald for his sins and treacherous deeds and offered to convert him to Islam as a way to repent. When Raynald staunchly refused, Saladin arose and cut off the man's head with his sword.

The Frankish prisoners of war faced various fates, depending on their ability to threaten Saladin. Average foot soldiers were taken to Damascus and sold as slaves. About two hundred knights, deemed to be the fiercest fighters, were decapitated at the sultan's command. Rather than use professional soldiers for the task, Saladin handed swords to the *mutawwiun*. However, the men were not used to committing violent acts, according

In Their Own Words

Sultan Saladin Reviews His Army

Before Saladin's army marched against the Franks, the sultan conducted a military review, described in poetic language by the Arab chronicler Ali Ibn al-Athir:

> On the day of the review the Sultan came forward to set the army in order, to divide it into sections and to draw up its ranks far and near. To every emir he assigned a duty, to every knight a post, to every lucky champion a station, to every ambush a place, to every combatant an opponent, to every burning spark someone to extinguish it, to every company (of Franks) someone to destroy it, to every flintstone someone to strike it, to every blade someone to whet it, to each action a command, to each arrow a point, to each right hand a sword, to each sword a hilt, to every courser [swift horse] an arena, to every outrider a defense, to every archer a target, to every leader a follower, to everything rising a place to which to rise, to every name an object. To each emir he assigned a place on the left or the right from which he was not to move, whence his body was not to absent itself, nor was any one of them to depart. He brought forward the front line of gallant archers of each battalion, advising each section of what would bring it into contact with another section. He said: "When we enter the enemy's terrain this is our army's battle order . . . the scene on which we shall be transfigured."

Quoted in Francesco Gabrieli, *Arab Historians of the Crusades*. New York: Routledge, 2010, pp. 75–76.

to al-Din: "There were some [executioners] who slashed and cut cleanly, and were thanked for it; some who refused and failed to act, and were excused; some who made fools of themselves, and others took their places . . . I saw how [they] killed unbelievers to give life to Islam."[64]

Jerusalem Falls

The walls and forts of Jerusalem were now left undefended, but Saladin did not attack. Without Frankish soldiers and governors, the Christian rule of the city collapsed with no blood being spilled. Saladin used his army to take control of port cities in and around Palestine, including Beirut, Haifa, and Jaffa.

Saladin's army did not march into Jerusalem until the end of September 1187. Rather than slaughter the Franks and plunder the town, Saladin gave Jerusalem's Christians forty days to buy their freedom at the cost of ten dinars. (By contrast, a good horse cost about one hundred dinars.) Those who did not pay would be taken captive and sold as slaves. According to al-Din, people employed various ruses to escape Jerusalem without paying for their freedom: "Some people were let down from the walls on ropes, some carried out hidden in luggage, some changed their clothes and went out dressed as [Muslim] soldiers."[65] Despite the relatively low price for freedom, about fifteen thousand of Jerusalem's Christians, including eight thousand women and children, were sold into slavery.

As Saladin and his army took control of Jerusalem, they set out to wipe away any signs of Christian rule. Crosses were ripped down and churches stripped of their treasures. Some were converted into mosques or madrassas. After eighty-eight years of Christian rule, the Holy Land had now been restored to Islam by the victories of Saladin's army over the crusaders. However, when news of Jerusalem's fall reached the West, English king Richard the Lionhearted organized the Third Crusade. Between 1189 and 1192, the Mamluks, Seljuks, Bedouins, Africans, and others would continue to spill blood, stage sieges, and fight to the death on open ground. The battle was won, but the Crusades would continue.

Chapter Five

Constantinople in Ruins: The Crusaders' Great Betrayal

At the end of the twelfth century, Constantinople was one of the richest and most culturally diverse cities in the world. The city was the capital of the Byzantine Empire and home to around four hundred thousand people who worshipped in temples, mosques, and churches that lined the streets. One of Constantinople's most stunning landmarks was, and still is, the Hagia Sophia, a soaring marble church decorated with gold, silver, ivory, pearls, and precious jewels. The church's immense golden dome was described by the sixth-century scholar Procopius as "a work admirable and terrifying . . . seeming not to rest on the masonry below it, but to be suspended by a chain of gold from the height of the sky."[66]

Innocent Launches the Fourth Crusade

The Crusades were launched in part to protect and defend Constantinople, the Byzantine Empire, and the Greek Orthodox Church. In the first years of the thirteenth century, the Latin warriors of the Fourth Crusade betrayed that promise. And they did so in the most violent and destructive manner possible, terrorizing the citizens of Constantinople, looting its riches, and reducing much of the city to smoldering ruins.

Oddly, when Pope Innocent III launched the Fourth Crusade in 1198, Constantinople was not even on the itinerary. Innocent called on the crusaders to invade Egypt, the chief center of Muslim power. The pope believed that by deposing the Egyptian sultan, Saphadin (Saladin's younger brother, who assumed power in 1193), Muslim rule over Jerusalem would crumble. However, the holy warriors of the Fourth Crusade never made it to Egypt or Jerusalem. Instead they attacked Constantinople and other medieval cities along the Adriatic Sea, an arm of the Mediterranean Sea east of Italy.

Sea Travel from Venice

The Fourth Crusade was a disaster from the start, marked by a shortage of money, materials, manpower, and leadership. Innocent originally set the date March 1, 1199, for the crusaders to depart for the Holy Land. But the date was pushed back several times. The expensive and lethal failures of earlier crusades left few European nobles willing to take up the cross, and the pope could not find the men he needed to fight. However, in 1200 a group of six French noblemen committed themselves to raising an army for the Fourth Crusade. They planned to launch the crusade from Venice, where ships would transport men, horses, and weapons down the Adriatic to port cities in Palestine.

Venice was the richest city in Europe and the only place where enough ships could be acquired to accommodate the crusaders. By this time few crusaders or Christian pilgrims walked the hazardous land route to the Holy Land; those who could afford it booked passage on ships. But sea travelers faced their own catalog of horrors on military galleys and transport ships.

> **WORDS IN CONTEXT**
> **galley**
> A long, slender ship commonly used on the Mediterranean Sea for warfare, propelled by fifty to sixty rowers wielding long oars.

A Terrifying Journey

Galleys were relatively small ships propelled by teams of rowers who labored belowdecks. The ships were slow and hard to maneuver in emergencies. Voyagers faced many dangers on the sea, including lightning strikes, groundings, and crashes into rocky reefs. People were swept overboard, and the ships sometimes burned from accidental fires caused by candles and cooking coals. Pirates were also a threat. Fulcher of Chartres describes the perils of sea travel:

> Many are the troubles which, God willing or permitting, meet those sailing at sea. . . . Many ships are accustomed to run into danger in the Gulf of Adalia [Turkey]. Here the winds blow in violently from all sides, down the mountains into the valleys to be deflected through gorges and converging into a whirlwind in the Gulf. If sometimes the mariners meet a pirate ship they are robbed and pitilessly ruined.[67]

The Hagia Sophia (pictured)—with its stunning marble walls and decorations of gold, silver, ivory, and pearls—was a befitting monument for Constantinople. The city was one of the richest and most culturally diverse in the medieval world.

Even if the sea was calm and pirates were few, ship travel was miserable and marked by shortages of food and water. According to British history professor Norman Housley, crusaders making a sea journey in the thirteenth century were advised to bring with them "six jars of butter, a leg of pork, a side of beef, and [a sack] of flour . . . but most of it would surely have become inedible in the heat of a Mediterranean voyage. . . . Drinking water became putrid and swarmed with worms."[68] Add to this hard beds, overcrowded ships, and hundreds of seasick, vomiting passengers and it is easy to understand why First Crusades historian Baldric of Bourgueil wrote that he was "terrified just looking at a map of the Mediterranean."[69]

Building Transports

Despite the dangers, Innocent and the crusading French lords laid out plans to obtain a large fleet of ships for the Fourth Crusade. They sent envoys to Venice in 1201 to negotiate with Enrico Dandolo, an executive called a doge who controlled shipping and trade in Venice. Dandolo was more than eighty-five years old and blind but extremely powerful. He had been elected to a lifetime post by a wealthy clique of Venice merchants. Dandolo laid out his terms to the French envoys:

> We will build transports for carrying 4,500 horses and 9,000 esquires, and other ships to accommodate 4,500 knights and 20,000 foot-soldiers. We will also include in our contract a nine month's supply of rations for all these men and fodder for all the horses. That is what we will do for you, and no less, on condition you pay us four marks per horse and two marks per man. . . . The total cost of what we have outlined here amounts to 85,000 marks.[70]

Although it is difficult to compare the value of medieval currency to modern money, it is estimated the doge was asking about $3,000 per horse and $1,500 per man. The terms of the agreement required the doge to suspend all overseas commerce in Venice for eighteen months. This would give merchants and shipbuilders time to gather supplies and manufacture numerous seaworthy vessels.

Looking Back

Shipbuilding in Venice

The Fourth Crusade would not have been possible without support from Venetian shipbuilders, as British military historian David Nicolle explains:

> Throughout the medieval period, the Venetian shipbuilding industry relied upon forests in the Istrian peninsula [in Croatia]. Great logs were then tied together to be floated along the coast to Venice, where most ships were constructed in private yards. These "private arsenals" were usually near the owner's home and provided employment when winter prevented fishermen from sailing. . . .
>
> The Venetian commitment to [shipbuilding] was massive, but it was not just the Venetian government's money that was involved; large numbers of ordinary people, from merchants to craftsmen, committed their labor and resources. It appears that an agreement to build a ship normally began with the formation of a partnership, with each partner having a share in the vessel. Skilled men would then be hired under one or more master craftsmen. . . . [Such] partners were often unable to pay all these costs without borrowing heavily, sometimes agreeing to repay their creditors out of profits from the ship's first voyage. The net result was that a large part of the Venetian population was depending upon the success of the Fourth Crusade.

David Nicolle, *The Fourth Crusade, 1202–04.* Oxford: Osprey, 2011, pp. 113–14.

The envoys returned home and asked crusading lords to raise the money necessary to meet Dandolo's demands. The pope used the power of the church to raise more money. He commanded that chests be placed in every parish church to receive gifts from the faithful, who were constantly urged in sermons to contribute as much as they could to the cause.

Short on Funds

The date of departure for the Fourth Crusade was set for June 29, 1202. Despite the pope's efforts and pledges by Venetians and others, only about 11,000 crusaders had arrived in Venice by June. The crusaders were short not only 22,500 soldiers but also money; Dandalo expected to receive 85,000 marks for services rendered, and the pope, aristocrats, and crusaders had only raised about 50,000 marks.

Whatever their numbers, the armed crusaders posed a problem for Venetians. The men ran up bills for food and lodging that they could not pay. The situation seemed likely to explode into violence. Many highly skilled French infantrymen were notoriously vicious mercenaries. They refused to go home unless they were at least paid for their travel.

> **WORDS IN CONTEXT**
>
> **excommunicate**
>
> An act of religious reprimand used to rescind membership in the church.

Eventually, a deal was made by Dandolo and the French nobles. Venice would make up for the monetary shortfall and provide the necessary ships and supplies. In return, the crusaders would conquer Zara (now called Zadar), a heavily fortified port city on the Dalmatian coast. After the crusaders pillaged Zara, they would share half the booty with Dandolo and the leaders of Venice.

Zara had once belonged to Venice but had fallen under Hungarian control in 1187. Residents of Zara ran a large trading empire in the Mediterranean Sea that was a direct economic threat to the merchants of Venice. Dandolo wanted to destroy this threat, but the crusaders were initially reluctant. Zara was a Christian city, and the Hungarian king, Emeric had taken vows to join the Fourth Crusade. Innocent forbade the attack on Zara, but the Frankish leaders felt they had little choice; if they did not take up the offer, they would be forced to return home penniless and humiliated. In early October 1202 the French barons finally signed the deal with Dandolo. They took control of a fleet of about 60 war galleys, 150 horse-transporting galleys, and 50 transport ships. The vessels were efficiently loaded with men, horses, siege engines, and provisions. (Several hundred other ships built for the crusade were unmanned, unpaid for, and left in Venice.) With local food supplies nearly gone, the crusaders set sail. Almost immediately, one of the largest vessels, the overloaded *Violet*, sank and drowned all on board except one knight who swam to safety.

Answering a Prince's Call

The crusaders reached Zara on November 10. They destroyed most of the city's walls and burned many of its buildings. Innocent was angered by this turn of events and excommunicated the entire crusading army, expelling each man from the church.

During the winter in Zara, the crusaders decided to invade Constantinople on their way to Egypt. The justification for the mission concerned a power struggle between members of the Byzantine emperor's family. The emperor, Isaac II, had been deposed, blinded, and imprisoned by his brother, Alexius. Isaac's nineteen-year-old son, also named Alexius, wished to restore his father to the throne. The prince promised the crusaders a huge sum, 200,000 marks, for their help. The pope was adamantly opposed to this plan and forbade the crusaders from invading Constantinople.

Ignoring the pope who had excommunicated them, the crusaders sailed for Constantinople in June 1203. The French knight and historian Geoffrey de Villehardouin describes the feelings of Christian crusaders when they arrived in Constantinople:

> You may be assured that those who had never seen Constantinople opened wide eyes now; for they could not believe that so rich a city could be in the whole world, when they saw her lofty walls and her stately towers wherewith she was encompassed, and these stately palaces and lofty churches, so many in number as no man might believe who had not seen them, and the length and breadth of this

Residents of Constantinople watch the arrival of the fleet of the Fourth Crusade in 1203. The crusaders who had pledged to defend the city instead destroyed it, terrorizing its citizens and looting its riches.

town which was sovereign over all others. And know that there was no man among us so bold but that his flesh crept at the sight.[71]

On July 5 contingents of Franks and Venetians began their invasion. Fully armed knights jumped into the waist-deep water with lances held high. They were followed by archers, crossbowmen, and peasant soldiers called sergeants. Thousands of horses were led off ships. Many were clad in full mail called barding, a new development meant to protect the horses from enemy arrows. The music played during the attack is described by French knight Robert de Clari:

> And they let sound trumpets of silver and of brass, as many as a hundred pair of them, and tabours [drums] and timbrels [tambourines] in great number. When the people of the city saw this great fleet, and heard the sound of the trumpets and the tabours, which made great noise, then did they arm themselves every one, and they went up upon the housetops and upon the towers of the city. Then in sooth [truth] did it seem to them that all the sea and the land trembled and that the whole sea was covered with ships.[72]

By Land and by Sea

The crusaders arrived with little warning, and the Byzantines were unprepared. Their army was short on fighters and relied on English, Danish, and French mercenaries. A few years before the Fourth Crusade, a Jewish merchant named Benjamin of Tudela (Spain) described the Byzantine military situation: "They hire from amongst all nations warriors to fight with the . . . Turks; for the natives are not warlike, but are as women who have no strength to fight."[73]

Even the professional soldiers who were hired to defend the city were frightened by the assembled Christian army; they fled before the crusaders could approach. The crusaders attacked on two fronts, from land and sea. For the land effort, the crusaders selected the northwestern corner of the city's fortified walls, where the emperor's home, the Blachernae Palace, was located. Benjamin describes the wealth within the palace:

> [The emperor] overlaid its columns and walls with gold and silver, and engraved thereon representations of the battles before his day and of his own combats. He also set up a throne of gold and precious stones, and a golden crown was suspended by a golden chain over the throne, so arranged that he might sit thereunder. It was inlaid with jewels of priceless value, and at night time no lights were required, for every one could see by the light which the stones gave forth.[74]

The crusaders took up positions near the palace for a siege. They erected tents, rolled siege engines into place, dug trenches, and built wooden palisades for protection. On July 12 close-range catapult bombardments began with the stones of the crusaders crashing into the emperor's palace. The defenders retaliated, launching stones and firebrands into the besieger's camp.

A second group of crusaders attacked from the harbor, aiming to destroy the long stretch of fortifications and defensive towers along Constantinople's harbor. The battle is described by Villehardouin:

> [The] attack was stiff and good and fierce. . . . At least fifteen got upon the wall, and fought there, hand to hand, with axes and swords, and those within redoubled their efforts and cast them out in very ugly sort. . . . Then might you have seen the mangonels shooting from the ships and transports, and the crossbow bolts flying, and the bows letting fly their arrows deftly and well; and those within defending the walls and towers very fiercely; and . . . the tumult and noise were so great that it seemed as if the very earth and sea were melting together.[75]

Constantinople Burns

Facing defeat, Emperor Alexius III fled the city with hundreds of pounds of gold and sacks full of imperial jewelry. The crusaders released the former emperor, Isaac II, from prison. His son was crowned coemperor Alexius IV in August. The new emperor had promised the crusaders great riches for their efforts but in reality had little money to pay them. To make good on his promise, Alexius IV began confiscating valuables from the Constantinople churches. This generated great hostility among the city's residents.

On August 18 angry Greek citizens started a riot, killing numerous western European residents who had lived in the city for years and who had previously supported the Byzantine emperor. The Westerners retaliated, starting a fire that grew into one of the greatest conflagrations in history up to that time. More than one hundred thousand people were left homeless.

In Their Own Words

Murderous Madmen Defile Constantinople

A Byzantine imperial court official named Nicetas describes the deeds of the crusaders as they raped, pillaged, and murdered in Constantinople on April 14, 1204:

> What then should I recount first and what last of those things dared at that time by these murderous men? O, the shameful dashing to earth of the venerable icons and the flinging of the relics and the saints, who had suffered for Christ's sake, into defiled places! . . .
>
> Did these madmen, raging thus against the sacred, spare pious matrons and girls of marriageable age or those maidens who, having chosen a life of chastity, were consecrated to God? . . . There were lamentations and cries of woe and weeping in the narrow ways, wailing at the crossroads, moaning in the temples, outcries of men, screams of women, the taking of captives, and the dragging about, tearing in pieces, and raping of bodies heretofore sound and whole. They who were bashful of their sex were led about naked, they who were vulnerable in their old age uttered plaintive cries, and the wealthy were despoiled of their riches. Thus it was in squares, thus it was on corners, thus it was in the temples, thus it was in the hiding places; for there was no place that could escape detection or that could offer asylum to those who came streaming in.

Quoted in Barbara H. Rosenwein, ed., *Reading the Middle Ages: Sources from Europe, Byzantium, and the Islamic World.* Toronto: University of Toronto Press, pp. 308–309.

Alexius IV was blamed for the tragedy, since he had invited the crusaders to Constantinople. In February 1204 the emperor was overthrown and strangled by Byzantine's next emperor, Alexius V. The new emperor met with the crusaders, hoping to negotiate their withdrawal from Byzantine territory. When no agreement was reached, the French forces and their Venetian allies made plans for a total conquest of Constantinople. They would have to fight the Byzantine soldiers and the mercenaries who had once again taken control of the city after Alexius IV came to power.

Crusaders Plunder and Rejoice

The crusaders launched the final siege of Constantinople on April 9, 1204. Contingents of combat engineers, called miners, dug tunnels under Constantinople's defensive sea walls, causing them to weaken. Related engineers called sappers carved trenches with crowbars and picks around walls. This work was meant to "sap" the strength of the fortifications. Sappers worked under wheeled defensive machines called cats, covered with animal hides. As they worked, Byzantine soldiers rained down rocks and firebrands. Every miner and sapper was killed. However, after extensive combat, the crusaders defeated the Byzantines and found themselves in uncontested control of Constantinople on April 13.

Following the battle, the holy warriors of the Fourth Crusade engaged in a frenzy of massacre, pillage, and destruction. More fires were set, which destroyed about one-sixth of the city. According to Villehardouin, "This was the third fire there had been in Constantinople since the Franks arrived in the land; and more houses had been burned in the city than there are houses in any three of the greatest cities in the kingdom of France."[76]

As Constantinople smoldered, residents buried their valuables in hastily dug holes. The city's aristocrats, religious leaders, and wealthy merchants loaded wagons with their most treasured possessions and tried to escape. Others surrendered to the crusaders with crosses and other

> **WORDS IN CONTEXT**
>
> **Latins**
>
> A term used for crusaders from France, Italy, and other western European regions.

religious icons held high. According to a Byzantine imperial court official named Nicetas, the religious symbols had little calming effect on the crusaders: "Instead, they plundered with impunity and stripped their victims shamelessly, beginning with their carts. Not only did they rob them of their substance but also the articles consecrated to God."[77]

As the conquerors took control of the city, the leaders moved into Blachernae Palace and a second royal residence called Bucoleon Castle. Both buildings were stripped of their riches. Other crusaders spread out through the city as troops took up residence in Constantinople's finest homes. Villehardouin describes the plundering:

> The booty gained was so great that none could tell you the end of it: gold and silver, and vessels and precious stones, and [luxurious fabric] samite, and cloth of silk, and robes fair and grey, and ermine, and every choicest thing found upon the earth. And well does Geoffrey of Villehardouin the Marshal of Champagne, bear witness, that never, since the world was created, had so much booty been won in any city . . . and greatly did they rejoice and give thanks because of the victory God had vouchsafed to them—for those who before had been poor were now in wealth and luxury.[78]

Slaughter of the Innocents

The rampaging crusaders robbed Constantinople's churches of relics, chalices, ornaments, silver railings, gold plates, and anything else they could load into wagons. They stripped altars, smashed icons, and pried jewels from sacred vessels. Thousands of art masterpieces were stolen, mutilated, or destroyed. Constantinople's great libraries were burned along with countless ancient manuscripts, some written in the third century BCE.

When not pillaging, the crusaders engaged in widespread murder and torture, killing priests, bishops, and monks. Women were forced to remove their clothing in case they might be hiding jewelry or other valuables. Nicetas describes the brutality: "They slaughtered the newborn, killed matrons, stripped elder women and outraged old ladies. They tortured the monks, they hit them with their fists and kicked their bellies, thrashing and rending their revered bodies with whips. . . . [Many] were dragged like

Crusaders celebrate as Baldwin IX, the Count of Flanders, is declared Emperor Baldwin I of Constantinople in 1204. Baldwin would be murdered within a year of taking the throne.

sheep and beheaded on the holy tombs, the wretched slew the innocent."[79]

On the second day of mayhem, the city's extensive wine cellars were looted. Drunken crusaders went on a rampage of rape, sparing no women—including nuns and virgins. Men who tried to stop the evil were stabbed, hacked to pieces, or decapitated. Upon hearing news of the rampage, Innocent expressed extreme disappointment:

> The Latins have given an example only of iniquity [evil] and the works of darkness. . . . These defenders of Christ who should have turned their swords only against the infidel, have waded through Christian blood. . . . They have been seen tearing away the silver plating in the altars, breaking them into fragments which they have disputed with each other, violating sanctuaries, and plundering icons, crosses, and relics.[80]

The End of the Crusades

On May 16, 1204, leader of the Fourth Crusade Baldwin IX, Count of Flanders, entered the lavish Hagia Sophia in Constantinople. Religious officials anointed Baldwin's body with sacred oils, then dressed him in a tunic with gold buttons. A heavy silk cloak, called a loros, was wrapped around his body, and a jewel-encrusted shroud, or chlamys, was placed on his shoulders. The chlamys was decorated with double-headed eagles embroidered in gold thread so bright it appeared to be aflame. Finely tooled red leather shoes were slid onto Baldwin's feet.

When properly attired, Baldwin was crowned the Latin emperor of Constantinople. A royal chain was placed around his neck and a gold crown on his head. As the crowd cheered, Emperor Baldwin I took a seat on a raised throne and waved his royal scepter high.

Baldwin I was the first Roman Catholic to become emperor of Constantinople, and by extension, the Byzantine Empire. But he was the sixth man within the past twelve months to be crowned Byzantine emperor. Of the five previous emperors, two were dead and three had fled to parts unknown.

With Baldwin I on the throne, the Fourth Crusade ended without a single battle against Muslim forces. Most crusaders returned home, brimming with riches. Although they had been banned from the church, their new wealth bought them official forgiveness; Innocent soon rescinded the blanket excommunication against the crusaders, providing they tithed some of their wealth to the church.

Baldwin himself would be murdered within a year of claiming the throne, and the Latin Empire of Constantinople he founded lasted little more than half a century. In 1261 Constantinople was once again reclaimed by the Byzantines. By that time the city, with its economy destroyed and it wealth plundered, was struggling to survive. Only about thirty-five thousand people remained in what had once been the shining center of power in the Byzantine Empire.

The Crusades continued until 1291, but like the sack of Constantinople, the fighting in the final years was driven more by the quest for wealth and power than religious belief. As with most wars, those who suffered most were innocent women, children, and the elderly, who had little to gain and much to lose. They would never replace the homes, schools, churches, and shops destroyed by war.

Source Notes

Introduction: What Were the Crusades?

1. Quoted in Elizabeth Hallam, ed., *Chronicles of the Crusades*. New York: Welcome Rain, 2000, p. 63.

Chapter One: Clash of Cultures

2. Jonathan Phillips, *The Crusades, 1095–1197*. Edinburgh Gate, UK: Pearson, 2002, p. 10.
3. Will Durant, *The Age of Faith*. Irvine, CA: World Library, 1994, p. 668.
4. Quoted in Alan Kendall, *Medieval Pilgrimages*. New York: Putnam, 1970, p. 30.
5. Durant, *The Age of Faith*, pp. 752–53.
6. Quoted in Michael J. O'Neal, *The Crusades Almanac*. Detroit: UXL, 2005, p. 54.
7. Quoted in Susanna A. Throop, *Crusading as an Act of Vengeance, 1095–1216*. Burlington, VT: Ashgate, 2011, p. 50.
8. Quoted in Guy Le Strange, *Palestine Under the Moslems*. Charlestown, MA: Acme Bookbinding, 2003, pp. 239–40.
9. Quoted in Norman P. Zacour and Harry W. Hazard, eds., *A History of the Crusades, vol. 5: The Impact of the Crusades on the Near East*. Madison: University of Wisconsin Press, 1985, p. 14.
10. Quoted in Thomas F. Madden, ed., *Crusades: The Illustrated History*. Ann Arbor: University of Michigan Press, 2004, p. 26.
11. Quoted in Bernard Lewis, *Islam: from the Prophet Muhammad to the Capture of Constantinople*, vol. 1. New York: Harper & Row, 1974, p. 55.
12. Thomas Asbridge, *The First Crusade*. Oxford: Oxford University Press, 2004, pp. 812–13.

Chapter Two: Crusaders March to the Holy Land

13. Fulcher of Chartres, *A History of the Expedition to Jerusalem, 1095–1127*, ed. Harold S. Fink. New York: Norton, 1969, p. 74.

14. Quoted in Richard L. Crocker, "Early Crusader Songs," Ohio State University Press, 2014. https://ohiostatepress.org.

15. Quoted in Jonathan Riley-Smith, ed., *The Oxford Illustrated History of the Crusades*. Oxford: Oxford University Press, 1995, p. 99.

16. Raymond d'Aguiliers, "Historia francorum qui ceperint Jerusalem," Internet Medieval Sourcebook, Fordham University, December 1997. www.fordham.edu.

17. D'Aguiliers, "Historia francorum qui ceperint Jerusalem."

18. D'Aguiliers, "Historia francorum qui ceperint Jerusalem."

19. Quoted in Norman Housley, *Fighting for the Cross*. New Haven, CT: Yale University Press, 2008, p. 93.

20. Quoted in Hallam, *Chronicles of the Crusades*, p. 85.

21. Quoted in August Charles Krey, ed., *The First Crusade: The Accounts of Eye-Witnesses and Participants*. Gloucester, MA: Peter Smith, 1958, p. 158.

22. Fulcher, *A History of the Expedition to Jerusalem*, p. 96.

23. Quoted in Asbridge, *The First Crusade*, p. 274.

24. D'Aguiliers, "Historia francorum qui ceperint Jerusalem."

25. D'Aguiliers, "Historia francorum qui ceperint Jerusalem."

26. D'Aguiliers, "Historia francorum qui ceperint Jerusalem."

27. Quoted in H.A.R. Gibb, ed., *The Damascus Chronicle of the Crusades*. Mineola, NY: Dover, 2002, p. 295.

28. Quoted in Housley, *Fighting for the Cross*, pp. 158–59.

29. Quoted in Hallam, *Chronicles of the Crusades*, p. 86.

30. James A. Brundage, *Law, Sex, and Christian Society in Medieval Europe*. Chicago: University of Chicago Press, 1990, p. 211.

Chapter Three: Crusaders Battle for Jerusalem

31. Quoted in Thomas Asbridge. *The Crusades: The Authoritative History of the War for the Holy Land*. New York: HarperCollins e-books, 2013, p. 121.

32. Fulcher, *A History of the Expedition to Jerusalem*, p. 117.

33. Ralph of Caen, *The Gesta Tancredi of Ralph of Caen*, trans. B.S. Bachrach and D.S. Bachrach. Burlington, VT: Ashgate, 2010, pp. 136–37.

34. Quoted in Asbridge, *The First Crusade*, p. 303.

35. Quoted in Hallam, *Chronicles of the Crusades*, p. 88.

36. Quoted in Hallam, *Chronicles of the Crusades*, p. 89.

37. Quoted in Asbridge, *The First Crusade*, p. 308.

38. Quoted in Susan B. Edgington, trans., *Albert of Aachen's History of the Journey to Jerusalem*, vol. 1. Burlington, VT: Ashgate, 2013, p. 213.

39. Quoted in Asbridge, *The First Crusade*, p. 309.

40. Quoted in Edgington, *Albert of Aachen's History of the Journey to Jerusalem*, p. 213.

41. Fulcher, *A History of the Expedition to Jerusalem*, p. 120.

42. Quoted in Krey, *The First Crusade*, pp. 259–60.

43. Quoted in Krey, *The First Crusade*, p. 260.

44. Quoted in Krey, *The First Crusade*, p. 261.

45. Asbridge, *The First Crusade*, p. 316.

46. Edgington, *Albert of Aachen's History of the Journey to Jerusalem*, p. 229.

47. Quoted in Internet Medieval Sourcebook, "The Siege and Capture of Jerusalem: Collected Accounts," Fordham University, December 1997. www.fordham.edu.

48. Quoted in Internet Medieval Sourcebook, "The Siege and Capture of Jerusalem."

49. Asbridge, *The First Crusade*, p. 318.

Chapter Four: Saladin's Army Defeats the Crusaders

50. Quoted in Asbridge, *The Crusades*, p. 428.

51. Quoted in Niall Christie, "A Translation of 'Ali ibn Tahir Al-Sulami," Cornell University, 2001. www.arts.cornell.edu.

52. Anna Comnena, "The Alexiad: Book I," Internet Medieval Sourcebook, Fordham University, February 2001. www.fordham.edu.

53. Quoted in R.C. Smail, *Crusading Warfare, 1097–1193*. Cambridge: Cambridge University Press, 1956, p. 78.

54. Quoted in Housley, *Fighting for the Cross*, p. 229.

55. Internet Medieval Sourcebook, "De Expugatione Terrae Sanctae per Saladinum: The Battle of Hattin, 1187," Fordham University, December 1997. www.fordham.edu.

56. Internet Medieval Sourcebook, "De Expugatione Terrae Sanctae per Saladinum."

57. Quoted in D.R.M. Peter, "The Battle of Hattin (1187): Four Accounts," De Re Militari, January 14, 2014. http://deremilitari.org.

58. Quoted in Francesco Gabrieli, *Arab Historians of the Crusades*. New York: Routledge, 2010, p. 73.

59. Quoted in Peter, "The Battle of Hattin (1187)."
60. Quoted in Asbridge, *The Crusades*, p. 569.
61. Quoted in Asbridge, *The Crusades*, p. 572.
62. Quoted in Gabrieli, *Arab Historians of the Crusades*, p. 74.
63. Quoted in Asbridge, *The Crusades*, p. 574.
64. Quoted in Asbridge, *The Crusades*, p. 576.
65. Quoted in Gabrieli, *Arab Historians of the Crusades*, p. 94.

Chapter Five: Constantinople in Ruins: The Crusaders' Great Betrayal
66. Quoted in Durant, *The Age of Faith*, p. 168.
67. Quoted in David Nicolle, *Essential Histories: The Crusades*. London: Osprey, 2001, p. 61.
68. Housley, *Fighting for the Cross*, p. 87.
69. Quoted in Housley, *Fighting for the Cross*, p. 88.
70. Quoted in M.R.B. Shaw, trans., *Joinville & Villehardouin: Chronicles of the Crusades*. Baltimore: Penguin, 1963, p. 33.
71. Quoted in Durant, *The Age of Faith*, pp. 772–73.
72. Quoted in D.R.M. Peter, "Robert of Clari's Account of the Fourth Crusade," De Re Militari, January 20, 2014. http://deremilitari.org.
73. Benjamin of Tudela, "The Itinerary of Benjamin of Tudela," Project Gutenberg, February 8, 2005. www.gutenberg.org.
74. Benjamin, "The Itinerary of Benjamin of Tudela."
75. Geoffrey de Villehardouin, "Memoirs, or Chronicle of the Fourth Crusade and the Conquest of Constantinople," Internet Medieval Sourcebook, Fordham University, April 1996. www.fordham.edu.
76. Villehardouin, "Memoirs, or Chronicle of the Fourth Crusade and the Conquest of Constantinople."
77. Quoted in Barbara H. Rosenwein, ed., *Reading the Middle Ages: Sources from Europe, Byzantium, and the Islamic World*. Toronto: University of Toronto Press, 2006, p. 308.
78. Villehardouin, "Memoirs, or Chronicle of the Fourth Crusade and the Conquest of Constantinople."
79. Quoted in Susan Wise Bauer, *The History of the Renaissance World*. New York: Norton, 2013, p. 180.
80. Quoted in Henry Treece, *The Crusades*. New York: Random House, 1963, p. 229.

For Further Research

Books

Elizabeth Hallam, ed., *Chronicles of the Crusades*. New York: Welcome Rain, 2000.

Samuel Harding, *The Story of the Middle Ages*. San Diego: Didactic, 2013.

Gary Jeffrey, *Crusades*. New York: Crabtree, 2014.

Don Nardo, *Medieval Knights and Chivalry*. San Diego: ReferencePoint, 2014.

Michael Riley and Jamie Byrom, *The Crusades: Conflict & Controversy, 1095–1201*. London: Hodder Education, 2013.

Qaiser M. Talib, *Salah Ad-Din and the Crusades*. London: Ta-Ha, 2012.

Websites

Crusades (www.history.com/topics/crusades). Hosted by the History Channel, this site features articles about the Crusades and videos with reenactments of dramatic events.

De Re Militari (http://deremilitari.org). This site, hosted by the Society for Medieval Military History, contains information about warfare in the Middle Ages and includes detailed articles about the Crusades and crusader battles and weapons.

Internet Medieval Sourcebook (www.fordham.edu/Halsall/sbook.asp). This website provides a collection of documents written between the third and fifteenth centuries that describe numerous aspects of the medieval era, from peasant life to eyewitness accounts of the Crusades.

Medieval Warfare (www.medievalwarfare.info). A site highlighting the weapons, armor, warfare, torture, and tactics of the crusaders and other fighters during the Middle Ages.

Middle Ages (www.lordsandladies.org). This site is dedicated to daily life in the Middle Ages and features pages about the Crusades, siege weapons, knights, kings, and the lives of women.

Timeline for the Crusades and Christian Holy War to c. 1350 (http:// usna.edu/Users/history/abels/hh315/crusades_timeline.htm). A detailed chronology of the Crusades, with full-color photos of medieval crusader artwork and links to specific events such as the siege of Jerusalem.

Virtual Israel Experience: Jerusalem—the Old City (www.jewishvirtu allibrary.org/jsource/vie/Jerusalem2.html). A detailed site concerning the history of Jerusalem's Old City. Dozens of pictures of historic sites provide views seen by Christians and Muslims as they battled for control throughout the Crusades.

Index

prostitution, 41

Qalanisi, Ibn al-, 38

Ralph of Caen, 36, 43
Ramadan, 25
Raymond IV of Toulouse, 30–31
Raymond of Tripoli, 65
Raynald of Châtillon, 62, 66
Richard I (king of England), 37
Richard the Lionhearted (English king), 68

Saladin (sultan of Egypt and Damascus), 56–57, **58**
  declares war on Crusaders, 62
  defeat of Franks by, 65–66
  makeup of armies of, 61–62
  review of army by, 67
  slave soldiers of, 59
Saphadin (Egyptian sultan), 70
scurvy, 38–39
Seljuk Turks, 12–13, 32
  expansion into Byzantine Empire, 11
  take control of Jerusalem, 12
  as warriors, 59, 61
serfs, 16
  freeing of, 20
sharia (Islamic law), 25
shilling, definition of, 34

siege
  definition of, 32
  of Jerusalem, 44–53
siege engines, 45–46, **46**
St. Stephen's Gate (Jerusalem), 50, 51
Sulami, Ali ibn Tahir al-, 57–58

Tancred (French marquis), 43
Tarfurs, 33, 36
Templo, Richard de, 62
Third Crusade, 37, 39, 68
  route of, **12**
Tower of David (Jerusalem), 42–43, **44**
troubadours, definition of, 29

Urban II (pope), 10, 13, 20
Usama (Arab chronicler), 40

Venice, 70
  shipbuilding in, 73
Villehardouin, Geoffrey de, 75–76, 78, 81

William of Tyre, 40, 61

Zacour, Norman P., 22
Zara (Dalmatian port city), 74
  siege of, 75

Picture Credits

Cover: Procession of Crusaders around Jerusalem, 14th July 1099, 1841 (oil on canvas), Schnetz, Jean Victor (1787–1870)/Château de Versailles, France/Giraudon/Bridgeman Images

Maury Aaseng: 12

© Corbis: 52

© Heritage Images/Corbis: 21

© Historical Picture Archive/Corbis: 71

© Richard T. Nowitz/Corbis: 64

Thinkstock Images: 8, 9

Fr.20124 f.331 The Looting of Jerusalem after the Capture by the Christians in 1099, illuminated miniature from a universal chronicle, 1440 (vellum), Jean de Courcy, (15th century)/Bibliotheque Nationale, Paris, France/Bridgeman Images: 17

A Muslim school (colour litho), English School, (20th century)/Private Collection/© Look and Learn/Elgar Collection/Bridgeman Images: 24

Fr 5594 f.19 The First Crusade of Peter the Hermit, from 'Passages faits Outremer' written by Sebastien Mamerot, c.1490 (vellum), French School, (15th century)/Bibliotheque Nationale, Paris, France/Bridgeman Images: 30

Ms 828 f.33r Siege of Antioch, from the Estoire d'Outremer (vellum), William of Tyre (c.1130–85)/Bibliotheque Municipale de Lyon, France/Bridgeman Images: 35

Funeral of Godfrey of Bouillon (c.1060–1100) in Jerusalem, 23rd July 1100, 1838 (oil on canvas), Cibot, Edouard (Francois Berthelemy Michel) (1799–1877)/Château de Versailles, France/Giraudon/ Bridgeman Images: 39

Street in front of the Tower of David, Jerusalem, c.1880–1900 (photochrom), Swiss Photographer, (19th century)/Palestine Exploration Fund, London, UK/Bridgeman Images: 44

Preparations for the assault on Jerusalem (fresco), Overbeck, Friedrich (1789–1869)/Casino Massimo, Rome, Italy/Bridgeman Images: 46

Syria, Damascus, Musee National de Damas 12th century, surrender of Richard I Lionheart before Saladin after Battle of Hattin (1187)/De Agostini Picture Library/G. Dagli Orti/Bridgeman Images: 58

Fleet of the Fourth Crusade arriving in Constantinople in 1203, Howat, Andrew (20th Century)/Private Collection/© Look and Learn/Bridgeman Images: 76

Baldwin IX, Count of Flanders, declared Emperor of Constantinople, 1204 (chromolitho), French School, (19th century)/Private Collection/© Look and Learn/Bridgeman Images: 82

About the Author

Stuart A. Kallen is the author of more than 250 nonfiction books for children and young adults. He has written on topics ranging from the theory of relativity to the art of animation. In addition, Kallen has written award-winning children's videos and television scripts. In his spare time he is a singer, songwriter, and guitarist in San Diego.